WRITING ON THE JOB

PRAISE FOR *WRITING ON THE JOB*

"Every page of this slim volume has a wealth of real-world experience distilled into actionable and sage advice. Note to those early in their careers—do yourself a favor and read this book now and carefully. It will return that modest investment several times over."

—Ashvin B. Chhabra, author of *The Aspirational Investor: Taming the Markets to Achieve Your Life's Goals*

"Communicating clearly and confidently is an essential career skill. *Writing on the Job* is a concise, accessible guide to business writing in today's workplace."

—Margaret Steen, UC Berkeley Extension business writing instructor

"Martha Coven delivers a concise, thoughtful book that provides useful learning for a lifetime. She demonstrates how to write with clarity and liveliness, all the while illuminating why it is important for connecting with your audience. Essential for young professionals and seasoned writers alike."

—Myles C. Thompson, founding publisher of Columbia Business School Publishing

"Ideas are the lifeblood of enterprise, but they only matter if communicated effectively. In this brief book, Martha Coven exemplifies this lesson by explaining how to write clearly and compellingly across all of today's forms of communication, from emails and memos to speeches and slide decks. The result is an 'elements of professional style' for the twenty-first century."

—Donald H. Chew, editor of the *Journal of Applied Corporate Finance*

"Concise and compelling communication has never been more crucial in the noisy digital age. Taking audience, messaging, and industry expectations into account, *Writing on the Job* provides expert advice intertwined with practical examples for professionals across all experience levels to thrive as more effective communicators."

—Rimjhim Dey, founder and owner of
DEY.Ideas + Influence

WRITING ON THE JOB

BEST PRACTICES FOR COMMUNICATING
IN THE DIGITAL AGE

MARTHA B. COVEN

PRINCETON UNIVERSITY PRESS

PRINCETON AND OXFORD

Published by Princeton University Press
41 William Street, Princeton, New Jersey 08540
6 Oxford Street, Woodstock, Oxfordshire OX20 1TR

press.princeton.edu

All Rights Reserved

Library of Congress Cataloging-in-Publication Data
Names: Coven, Martha B., 1972– author.
Title: Writing on the job : best practices for communicating in the digital age / Martha B. Coven, Princeton University Press.
Description: Princeton, NJ : Princeton University Press, [2022] |
Includes bibliographical references and index.
Identifiers: LCCN 2021042258 (print) | LCCN 2021042259 (ebook) |
ISBN 9780691229959 (paperback) | ISBN 9780691229966 (ebook)
Subjects: LCSH: Business writing. | Business communication.
Classification: LCC HF5718.5 .C69 2022 (print) | LCC HF5718.5 (ebook) |
DDC 808.06/6658—dc23/eng/20211103
LC record available at https://lccn.loc.gov/2021042258
LC ebook record available at https://lccn.loc.gov/2021042259

British Library Cataloging-in-Publication Data is available

Editorial: Peter Dougherty and Alena Chekanov
Production Editorial: Kathleen Cioffi
Text Design: Carmina Alvarez
Cover Design: Karl Spurzem
Production: Erin Suydam
Publicity: Maria Whelan and Kathryn Stevens
Copyeditor: Jennifer McClain

This book has been composed in Minion Pro

Printed on acid-free paper. ∞

Printed in the United States of America

1 3 5 7 9 10 8 6 4 2

To the friends, family, students, and colleagues to whom I confessed the dream of writing this book. You know who you are, and I'm grateful to each of you for your support.

Contents

Writing for Public Audiences

WRITING ON THE JOB

Introduction

Writing is an essential skill in today's economy. We rely on words more than ever in the digital-age workplace, on messaging platforms and social media as well as in classic forms like memos and reports. And given how much reading is done on mobile devices, being able to write succinctly is critical to workplace success.

Clear and direct language—free of needless words and jargon—improves communication within an organization and supports informed decision-making. People who write well on the job are more effective at carrying out their organization's mission and more likely to advance professionally.

The primary audience for this book is professionals in the first decade of their careers, whether in the corporate world, at a non-profit organization, or in the public sector. If you are one of these people, you may still be developing the skill of writing an effective email communication, a persuasive memo, or a compelling slide deck. If you struggle with the fundamentals of writing, you may not be ready for this book. But if you can string together sentences and are looking for ideas on how to make your writing more accessible and powerful, *Writing on the Job* is for you.

This book will also be useful to people further along in their careers who find themselves with new responsibilities—or new communications platforms—to navigate. For example, the book explains how to write for social media and advises on tasks assigned to managers and executives, such as providing critical feedback through performance reviews or delivering a speech.

This book draws on my own experiences writing on the job for more than twenty-five years, in the White House and on Capitol Hill as well as in the private sector. It also relies on techniques I've developed in the classroom at Princeton University, where I train young professionals to write clearly and effectively. The book begins with the basics: how to develop a professional style, get started on a piece of writing, create a first draft, and edit it into a strong final product. It then offers advice on more than a dozen forms of writing, from a one-line tweet to a lengthy report, using concrete examples and templates. The book also provides guidance on how formal or informal to allow your language to be, and how to strike the right tone so your message gets heard. Throughout, it emphasizes the "bottom line up front" approach used by the US military to ensure efficient communications.

The goal is to help you write effectively on the job—and enjoy doing it!

The Basics

Developing a Professional Style

Writing on the job is different from texting or emailing friends and family, but it's not as different as you might imagine. Your writing will be more readable and enjoyable if you apply the natural voice you bring to personal communications. Your goal should be to sound lively, not stuffy. Writing in a professional style also involves being smart about how you use the page or screen, including by relying on formatting tools like bullets and bold print. If most of your reading consists of fiction or lengthy technical articles, which rarely use these tools, you may need to broaden your notion of what good writing looks like. Most importantly, good professional writing requires that you adjust to your audience. If you are coming from a school setting, your writing may have taken the form of a brain dump, where your goal was simply to demonstrate your mastery of a subject to an instructor. Or you may be in the habit of expressing yourself creatively, without a particular audience in mind. In the workplace, there's always an audience. Before beginning any writing task, it's critical to consider who they are, what they know, and what they care about.

Aim for Lively, Not Stuffy

People often make the mistake of thinking that serious writing is supposed to be wordy, dense, and stuffy. It should be just the opposite. You can write crisp, lively sentences and paragraphs and still come across as professional. Moreover, people will be more likely to read and appreciate what you have written.

If you're not sure how lively your writing should be, study the work of others. If you're writing on an internal messaging platform, look at how colleagues you admire express themselves. If you're writing your first internal memo or client report, ask for examples of others that have been well received. Don't feel bound to imitate them, but use them as a guide.

One way to make your writing lively is to use a variety of words, rather than relying on the same ones over and over. Look for ways to make your writing more compelling, which you can do without exaggerating. For example, describe a discovery as "jarring" instead of "surprising," or say you will "tackle" a project instead of "starting" on it.

Lively writing is one thing; being disrespectful is another. Stop yourself before you write something that could come across as snarky or demeaning. Not only can that be damaging in the moment, but your words will likely be preserved digitally, even in what feels like a passing virtual conversation, and may come back to haunt you. Even your personal communications can have workplace consequences. My rule of thumb is that if I feel at all uncomfortable as I write something, it's a sign that I need to find different words or hold back altogether.

If you are a manager, here are two additional notes of caution. First, pay particular attention to how you communicate, because you speak through a megaphone whether you realize it or not. Your words are taken seriously by your employees, and tone matters. Second, there is a fine line between communicating in a lively and engaging manner, which you absolutely should strive for, and coming across as juvenile or flippant, which may result in your losing the respect of your team—or even legal consequences.

Be Smart about How You Use the Page

One of the biggest differences between academic or creative writing and writing in a professional workplace is in how to use the page (or the screen). The key in professional writing is to avoid long blocks of text and to make strategic use of bullets or other formatting cues that help the reader navigate what you've written. You're much more likely to get your information and ideas across if they're presented in bite-size pieces. Using bold print or underlining can help point the reader to key terms or text within a sentence or paragraph, so long as you don't overdo it.

Compare the two texts below. The content is the same, but the formatted version is easier to read and would be entirely appropriate in a professional piece of writing.

This book presents guidance for professionals on a range of topics, including how to prepare visuals. The chapter on creating a slide deck suggests following a simple structure. The deck should begin with an opening slide, followed by an agenda slide. Next, the deck should include a series of slides with the core content, separated by transition slides. It should wrap up with a conclusion and next steps slide. The author suggests that when designing your slides, you should consider crafting informative titles, using a consistent format, limiting the use of text-only slides, leaving blank space, using color and symbols for emphasis, and disclosing original sources.

This book presents guidance for professionals on a range of topics, including how to prepare visuals. The chapter on **creating a slide deck** suggests following this simple structure:

1. opening slide
2. agenda slide
3. slides with core content, separated by transition slides
4. conclusion and next steps slide

When designing slides, the author suggests:

- crafting informative titles,
- using a consistent format,
- limiting use of text-only slides,
- leaving blank space,
- using colors or symbols for emphasis, and
- disclosing original sources.

While you can't chop up an entire memo or report into bullets, using them periodically will make your document more readable. Bullets can be effective in emails as well, when used to lay out information or list tasks.

Consider Your Audience

Your purpose in writing at work is to communicate to other people. You may be simply conveying facts, or you may be seeking to persuade. Either way, it's not about you; it's about them. Before beginning any piece of writing, ask yourself three questions.

1. **Who is your audience?** This will help you decide what vocabulary to use, what information to provide, and how to frame your arguments. Keep in mind that most adults in the US are not highly proficient readers. Online tools like the Hemingway App can help you assess the reading level of your writing, and a good rule of thumb is to stick to the eighth-grade level or below. Even if your audience is a well-educated group of professionals, they will appreciate your keeping things simple. This paragraph, for example, is written right around that eighth-grade level. Some of the most memorable speeches are written at a fourth-grade level.

2. **What does your audience know?** Consider what information your audience is likely to have on your topic. It may be none, or it may be substantial. If your audience is not very knowledgeable, one way to overcome your expertise and avoid technical jargon is to imagine you're explaining the issue to a family member or neighbor. Warren Buffett always wrote the annual Berkshire Hathaway shareholder letter as if the audience were his sisters, who did not work in finance. Even if your audience does have substantial background knowledge, it can still be useful to provide some brief context before you plunge into your core content. While you have been thinking about this topic, your readers have likely been focusing on other matters and could use help getting their heads into the issue. That said, your purpose should not be to convey everything you know, but rather to identify and share the information your audience needs. It's fine to be selective, so long as you

are not hiding critical facts or perspectives that would change the conclusion your reader might draw.

3. **What does your audience care about?** If you're trying to persuade your audience, figuring out what they care about is particularly important. Memos to executives will be more effective if you explain how your proposal advances their priorities, which could be profitability, customer or employee satisfaction, the company's reputation, or even an executive's reputation. You may need to feature these arguments more than others you find more compelling. You're already persuaded, after all. Your audience is what matters.

If you're trying to inform a broader audience about an issue you feel is important, consider what will make your readers care as much as you do. Are they concerned about implications for the economy? Their personal health or safety? Ask yourself what will resonate most and highlight that angle.

If your audience is seeking information to solve a problem or answer a question, make sure to address their needs directly. Good writing anticipates and answers the reader's questions.

Finally, take care to avoid language that could alienate your audience. There are good reasons to be sensitive to language choice, particularly on topics like race and gender. And words can have different meanings when communicating across cultures or countries. There is also a strong business case for being thoughtful in your word choice. Advertising executives Kenneth Roman and Joel Raphaelson, in their book *Writing That Works*, suggest making "a conscious effort not to insult people—nor offend, nor upset them—unwittingly and by accident. It is good business as well as good manners. Why rile up your customer or your client or your prospect?"

2

Getting Started

Getting started can be the hardest part of a writing project. Even accomplished authors confess to writer's block. Stephen King observed in his memoir that "the scariest moment is always just before you start."

Why does this happen? Sometimes we're stuck at the starting gate because we have too many thoughts swirling through our minds and don't know exactly what we want to say or where to begin. Or we hover over our computers, paralyzed because we can't produce the perfect sentence. Sound familiar? The strategies in this chapter and in chapter 3 get you going and help you produce a solid first draft, whether you're writing a two-paragraph email to a client or a three-page memo to the boss. Chapter 4 then provides practical tips for how to edit that draft into a polished final product.

Start Early

Procrastination is a writer's worst enemy. Whenever possible, build in enough time to walk away from a draft and come back to it with fresh eyes. Even shorter pieces of writing, like emails and social media posts, will be stronger if you wait 10 minutes before rereading and finalizing them. "Go away from it," Nobel laureate Toni Morrison once advised, then "read it as though it is the first time you've ever seen it."

Avoid Distractions

Turn off phone or email alerts that might distract you, and don't let yourself drift into scrolling through social media. If those conditions sound like writer's prison to you, set a time limit. Tell yourself you will write for 20 minutes, and then give yourself permission to take a break to check email or make a call. Once you get going, you may find you don't need that break. But knowing it's an option will help you relax and focus.

Use Your Voice

Talking and writing achieve the same objective, which is to communicate with words. Yet talking comes much more easily to us. If you are struggling to get words onto the page, talk through what you're trying to say with a colleague or in front of a mirror.

If you're not sure you'll remember what you said, record yourself and use the transcription as your starting point. We tend to speak in run-on, sloppy sentences, so you'll have to edit that language substantially. But it will get you going.

Prepare a Bullet Outline

Beginning with a brief outline solves the blank page problem and organizes your thoughts. An outline doesn't need to be formal or use Roman numerals. You can simply write out short bullets with the main points you want to get across. They don't need to be complete sentences, and you can ignore grammar and spelling. Just spill onto the page the ideas bouncing around in your head.

If even that feels difficult, take a walk down the hallway or step outdoors for some fresh air. As your head starts to clear, think about what you're trying to communicate, and the key points will come into focus.

After you have gotten your main points down, identify the most important ones. If you're writing a longer document like a memo or report, these points can become your headings. Nest beneath them less critical points that support another argument or illustrate a concept. Then think about which points should go first, to grab your reader's attention or frame the rest of the argument.

Once you have a bullet outline, you are ready to begin writing.

3

Writing a First Draft

Now that you've gotten started, here are five strategies for creating a solid first draft.

State the Bottom Line Up Front

There is no place for mystery in a document written on the job. Leave the suspense-building to the fiction writers. State your conclusion right away—or as they say in the military, bottom line up front (BLUF). The US Department of Defense is the largest employer in the world. Its leaders know that good writing can save time, money, and even lives.

Stating the bottom line up front is particularly important in the digital age, when you may only have a single screen to communicate. You can't count on readers to keep scrolling down. Journalists use an "inverted pyramid" structure for similar reasons. They can't assume their readers will stay with them to the end, so they put the essential information in the first paragraph (the who/what/when/where/why) and provide supporting details later in the story.

If you need the reader to take action, put that in your BLUF paragraph too, along with any relevant deadlines. You don't want to risk critical information getting buried and missed.

The one time when BLUF may not be appropriate is when you are delivering critical feedback, a topic discussed more fully in chapter 8.

Use Headings

Headings are a gift to the reader. They make it easier to navigate a document and skim back over it later. Luckily, if you have written a bullet outline, you have already created a first draft of your headings and subheadings.

The federal plain language guidelines, which advise government agencies on how to make their writing easier for the public to understand, describe three types of headings:

1. Statement headings ("Headings Help Guide a Reader")

2. Question headings ("Why Do We Use Headings?")

3. Topic headings ("Headings")

Statement headings are usually the best choice, because they convey the most information. A reader could scan through your document, looking only at the headings, and still grasp your main points. Most readers do, in fact, skim through materials in this manner, particularly when they are reading online. Numerous eye-tracking studies have found an F-shaped pattern, where readers start by looking briefly across the top line of the page and then drop down, scanning for another place to stop and read again, which a header can provide.

Question headings can be useful in documents whose purpose is to answer specific questions your client or customer may have. A troubleshooting guide, for example, might be written with question headings. Avoid topic headings, unless you are using them to label the sections of a longer document (such as "Executive Summary").

Always construct your headings in a parallel manner. You can use full sentences, fragments that start with a verb, or fragments that start with a noun. Just don't mix and match.

Your headings should also use the same language that appears in your BLUF opening, and present information in the same order. This isn't a place for creative variation, which will just confuse your reader. You want the BLUF paragraph to serve as a road map to what follows, and consistently crafted headings will aid in that journey.

Leave Blanks as You Write

It's natural to get stuck at various points as you write. Focus on the parts of your document you feel ready to tackle, and take advantage of any bursts of inspiration. A bullet outline makes this possible, because you can skip around without losing sight of the overall structure.

If you do leave blanks to fill in later, develop a clear way to mark them, so you don't overlook them when you are finalizing your document. For example, you could insert a string of X's that you can search for later, or highlight a block of placeholder text (such as "insert quarterly report data here") to serve as a reminder of what's missing.

Keep Your Sentences and Paragraphs Short

Keeping your sentences and paragraphs on the short side makes your document more readable. It's also essential for any communication likely to be read on a small screen, where large blocks of text appear particularly deadly. That said, a paragraph consisting entirely of short sentences would sound awkward. The real magic comes from varying the length of your sentences.

Gary Provost illustrated this point beautifully in his book *100 Ways to Improve Your Writing*:

> I use short sentences. And I use sentences of medium length. And sometimes when I am certain the reader is rested, I will engage him with a sentence of considerable length, a sentence that burns with energy and builds with all the impetus of a crescendo, the roll of the drums, the crash of the cymbals— sounds that say listen to this, it is important.
>
> So write with a combination of short, medium, and long sentences. Create a sound that pleases the reader's ear. Don't just write words. Write music.

Consider using commas to break up your longer sentences. Best-selling author Lynne Truss explains that a comma "tells the reader how to hum the tune." Compare these two sentences—can you hear the music better in the second one?

> The executive team decided to invest in a new marketing campaign which was designed to bring in additional customers such as large suppliers in the region who hold the key to growth for our company.

> The executive team decided to invest in a new marketing campaign, which was designed to bring in additional customers such as large suppliers in the region, who hold the key to growth for our company.

You can smooth the flow between shorter sentences with the help of transition words and phrases like **In addition**, **Finally**, **For example**, **Furthermore**, and **However**. These are signposts that help the reader follow your thinking. Phrases like "**There are three reasons why**" are also useful ways to set up and structure a paragraph, so the reader knows what's coming.

If you find yourself writing long paragraphs, consider breaking them in two, or present some of the text in a bulleted or numbered list. One of the dangers of long paragraphs, in addition to their unattractiveness, is that information gets lost. This is a particular risk if the information is buried in the middle of a long paragraph, which readers may skim past. Text at the beginning or end of a paragraph is more likely to be read.

Illustrate Your Ideas

It is far easier to understand an idea or an argument if it has been illustrated with a concrete example. Abstract concepts or claims are difficult to wrap our minds around. Examples help bring them to life.

For example (see?), consider this description of two formulas for measuring inflation, which would be more challenging to grasp without the fruit example in the middle.

The traditional formula used to calculate inflation does not account for substitution between product categories, even though consumers frequently make such substitutions. **For example, if the price of apples goes up while the price of bananas does not, some people will buy fewer apples and more bananas.** The alternative measure allows for this type of substitution.

The best illustration is one the reader can relate to on a personal level, like the choice between apples and bananas. So rather than talking about how your business assists its clients as a whole, share a brief story about how you solved a particular client's problem. Instead of talking about a group of people affected by a policy, share a vignette about one family. Your reader can imagine being that client or a member of that family much more easily than being in a faceless crowd.

If you don't have a ready-made example, use a hypothetical. For example, if you're analyzing the effects of reducing customer service staffing levels, you can make the consequences more real by adding an illustration like this: "Picture a working parent who calls at 9 p.m. and encounters wait times of an hour or more, cutting into precious time they'd set aside to pay bills or catch up on sleep. They won't feel kindly about our company if we do that to them."

A simple analogy or metaphor also can help communicate your idea. Two good places to look for inspiration are pop culture and the world of sports. For example, if you're arguing for keeping a low profile on a company activity, you might say, "We're not trying to be the Kardashians here. Let's keep this out of the spotlight." President Obama often made the case for steady, incremental progress by talking about "moving the ball down the field," or by noting that baseball teams win games by hitting singles and doubles, not just home runs.

Just be sure you're choosing a reference that won't leave your readers scratching their heads. The key is to tap into a shared experience or understanding. For example, researchers vividly illustrated the health risks of social isolation by explaining that it could be as damaging as smoking fifteen cigarettes a day. That's a concept any audience could readily grasp because the risks of smoking are well understood.

Considering your audience may help you identify the best analogy or metaphor. The Irish musician Bono persuaded religious conservatives to support efforts to combat the HIV/AIDS crisis at the turn of the century by describing it as "the leprosy of our age," tapping into a biblical frame of reference that was familiar and compelling to his audience.

4

Editing

Edit everything. Even a one-paragraph email. Your reputation as a professional is made and remade every time someone encounters your work, so you want your writing to be clear, succinct, and free of errors. Some people write more polished first drafts than others, but even the most talented writers set aside time to do a careful edit after they have completed a draft. Editing is also often necessary to reduce a draft to the appropriate length.

How long will it take you to edit? A good rule of thumb is to spend two-thirds of your time writing, and one-third editing. If it took you 10 minutes to write an email, allow another 5 minutes to review and edit it. If it took you two days to write a report, devote a third day to editing.

This chapter provides techniques for breaking the curse of the screen (where your writing looks deceptively polished), identifying needless or confusing words, making sure your writing is accurate and free of mistakes, and getting helpful feedback from someone else on your draft.

Get Away from the Screen

Screens can create challenges when it's time to edit. They make everything look tidy and professional, and trick us into thinking our work is polished and ready to go. We also read too quickly on a screen, because we tend to scroll. Editing requires a careful, slower read. Here are four techniques for breaking the curse of the screen— experiment to see which works best for you.

- **Print out a hard copy.** Even if you're comfortable with on-screen editing, it's smart to review a hard copy before you finalize your document. Your eyes may have flicked over the same mistake on the screen so many times that you no longer see it, but it may pop out once you see it on paper.

- **Read your writing aloud.** You can do this for a paragraph you're struggling with, to spot the awkward parts that need to be rewritten. Or read the full document aloud as a final check before you submit it, whether it's a short email or a longer report. I do this for everything I write that feels important. Reading out loud slows down your review, since we read twice as fast as we speak, and inevitably you will find something to fix.

- **Try to summarize what you have written.** This is a humbling but effective technique. Reread what you have written and then try to summarize it briefly, stating the key takeaway points. If that proves difficult, you have not been clear enough in your writing. And if your takeaway points are not the same as your headings, you need to do some restructuring. On the bright side, you now know what to emphasize as you edit and rewrite.

- **Copy what you have written by hand.** Take a paragraph you think needs editing, and copy it onto a sheet of paper. Writing by hand will smoke out needless words and confusing sentences, because your brain will get stuck on that language and your writing will slow down.

"Omit Needless Words! Omit Needless Words!
Omit Needless Words!"

In author E. B. White's introduction to the classic *The Elements of Style*, he explains that his college professor, Will Strunk, stripped so many needless words from his lectures that he frequently had time left to kill. Strunk's solution, says White, was to repeat each sentence three times. In a lecture on brevity,

Strunk "leaned forward over his desk, grasped his coat lapels in his hands, and, in a husky, conspiratorial voice, said, 'Rule Seventeen. Omit needless words! Omit needless words! Omit needless words!'"

The young E. B. White was soaking up that wisdom more than a century ago, but it remains useful today. If you do nothing else when you edit, omit needless words.

How do you find these needless words? Start by striking the word **that** wherever possible. This is a trick journalists use. Sometimes you'll need to keep it, but you'll be surprised how often you can remove it. Another offender is **the fact that**, which you should delete whenever you can, along with its cousin, "in fact." You may not need to replace it, but if you do, swap in a simple "because" or "although" for phrases like "due to the fact that" or "despite the fact that."

Next, look for qualifiers, which are words or phrases we sprinkle into our writing to hedge our bets but that rarely add meaning. These words can occasionally be useful—you'll find a few in this book, even—but they're needed far less often than you might think. Here are some qualifiers to consider cutting from your draft.

Words that suggest uncertainty:
apparently
basically
essentially
fairly
generally
I believe/feel/guess/think
in many ways
in my opinion
kind of
maybe
perhaps
practically
probably

    reasonably
    relatively
    seemingly
    somewhat
    sort of
    typically
    usually
    virtually

Words that suggest a larger amount:
    extremely
    highly
    a lot
    overly
    pretty
    quite
    rather
    really
    so
    too
    totally
    very

Words that suggest a smaller amount:
    a bit
    a little
    slightly

Then there are the words with a simpler alternative, including:
    for the purpose of (vs. for)
    in the event that (vs. if)
    in order to (vs. to)
    is capable of being (vs. can be)
    prior to (vs. before)
    subsequent to (vs. after)
    until such time as (vs. until)

Look out for other heavy-handed or awkwardly formal language, such as:

at the present time
at your earliest convenience
be advised that
bear in mind that
in accordance with
it goes without saying that
it is important/interesting/critical/worthwhile to note that
it should be pointed out that
of course
pursuant to
with reference to
with regard to

Once you've zapped as many needless words from your draft as you can, look for ways to sharpen the focus on the core content of your sentences. Here are three tactics to consider.

- **Check to see if the subject and verb both appear within the first eight words**. If they don't, the sentence will be harder to process. Compare these two sentences:

  While inserting long clauses into your writing allows you to share more of your thinking with your reader and helps you pack in additional content, you risk making your writing difficult to read.

  You risk making your writing difficult to read when you insert long clauses, even if they allow you to share more of your thinking.

  The rewritten sentence is easier to read, and putting the subject and verb ("you risk") first helps surface needless words to cut.

- **Tighten up your verbs.** I recently drafted an email that included the sentence "I have a client who has asked me to travel next week." I did a quick edit before sending it, trimming it down to "My client asked me to travel next week," which deleted four of the original twelve words.

- **Look for sentences or clauses that begin with a weak phrase like "there are" or "this is."** For example, instead of saying "There are customers saying this is a product that should be upgraded," you can simply write "Customers are asking for an upgrade."

Examine the beginning and end of your document, and you may find whole sentences of needless words. We have a habit of "throat-clearing" when we start writing, rather than jumping right in. For example, we say things like "You may be wondering why I am writing to you today." Delete that sentence. Go straight to "I'm writing to ask for your help with _____." Similarly, we often don't know when to end. Try taking what you have written and striking the first and last sentences. If that helps, try striking the second and second-to-last sentences. You may need to do a little rewriting to add polish or the right tone, but you're getting rid of a bunch of needless words.

Finally, as important as it is to declutter your writing, it is possible to go too far. If you tend to write short, clipped sentences, you may be among the minority of writers who need to add words as they edit, rather than striking them. You may want to combine two sentences into one longer one (by inserting "and" or "but") to create the variation in sentence length that makes writing more readable, or add a whole sentence if you've taken a logical leap and need to fill in that gap for your reader.

Prune Out the Jargon

Trimming needless words out of your writing makes it crisper. To make it clearer, you have to prune out the jargon. We often use jargon because we think it will impress our reader. In reality, it can make it more difficult to understand what we are saying and frustrate the reader.

A terrific way to spot jargony words and phrases is to read your writing aloud. The jargon will catch in your throat, because we simply would never say these words out loud. Why not? Either because they sound pretentious or because neither we nor the people we're addressing know exactly what they mean. When we speak, we are more focused on getting our meaning across because the audience is right in front of us and we can see the confusion on their faces when we aren't clear.

Here are the types of jargon to look out for as you edit.

Technical jargon. Whether to use technical jargon is a question of audience. Technical jargon can be appropriate if you are writing to colleagues inside your organization or within your field, if they are all familiar with the meaning of a term. Scientists writing for a scholarly journal, for example, should not hunt around for a plain language alternative to a well-known technical term that precisely captures a concept; doing so might even hamper their effort to communicate clearly.

However, using technical jargon risks discouraging and confusing any audience that includes nonexperts. If you're not sure whether your reader will understand a term but you desperately want to use it, explain it the first time it appears in your text. You should also ask yourself the hard question of whether you fully understand the meaning. When you spot technical jargon in your writing, try to define it on the spot. If you struggle, cut it and use plain English instead.

Business jargon ("bizspeak"). This is a tricky area to navigate. Bizspeak includes new words and phrases—often inspired by technological advances—that can be useful but may not be welcomed by older audiences. These words didn't appear in our childhood dictionaries, and may not even appear in today's dictionaries. The English language is always evolving, but it takes time for words to be widely accepted.

Here's my view. It's okay to use some bizspeak if (1) it won't irritate your audience; (2) your meaning is clear; and (3) you don't overuse it, to the point of sounding clichéd. I use terms like "value-add," "bandwidth," or "deliverables," particularly when writing to colleagues who share that vocabulary. These words have become popular because they are useful. Just don't overdo it. If you lean too hard on phrases like "thinking outside the box" or "paradigm shift," you probably haven't thought deeply enough about what you're trying to communicate.

Unnecessary abbreviations. It is tempting to use abbreviations because they save so much space. Why keep writing out the full name of something when you can use a few capital letters (AFCL) to abbreviate it instead?

Here's why you shouldn't use AFCL. Because you will irritate your readers if you insist that they remember what AFCL stands for and write AFCL every time you refer to the concept of using AFCL. Have you looked back at the previous paragraph yet to remind yourself what AFCL stands for? Are you annoyed? Exactly.

Abbreviations should be used only when they are well known to your readers. You can test for this by considering whether to write out the full name once before you start abbreviating. If you suspect you should write it out the first time, don't abbreviate it. It means your reader won't necessarily be familiar with the abbreviation, and may stumble on it when reading the rest of your document.

If the term you want to abbreviate is long, and it feels painful to write it out every time, shorten it by selecting a few words to stand in for the full term after you've stated it the first time. For example, the Leadership Conference on Civil and Human Rights is often referred to as the Leadership Conference.

Abstract words. The final type of jargon to look out for is abstract words. These are words that attempt to capture a big concept, but in such a simplistic way that the reader is left unsure of the writer's meaning. Abstract words also make for dull reading, because they lack the sparkle of more descriptive language.

Abstract words come in many forms, but the nouns often end in **-ion** and the verbs in **-ize**, so start by looking for those. Here's an example from a writing sample I was once given. See how many abstract words you can spot, and note how difficult this sentence is to process.

> To remove barriers to interconnectivity, we will provide capacity assistance for modernization and reforms that include harmonization and synchronization of policies, regulations, and institutional frameworks.

There is some meaning behind each of the -ion/-ize words, but because they are such broad terms, it's difficult to pinpoint that meaning. The sentence is tough to get through, because the reader has to stop at each abstract word and consider what is meant by it.

Use these words sparingly, and when you do, couple them with a concrete explanation. Don't just talk about modernizing or harmonizing; describe how a situation will change. Reducing your reliance on the shorthand of abstract words may make your writing longer, but it will become much more readable.

Think Like a Critic

After we've spent time writing something, we get attached to it, which can lead to blind spots when editing. One of the best ways to shake off that perspective is to imagine that the reader does not like you and does not trust you. Become your own worst critic.

As you read through your writing, stop every time you have stated a fact or made an argument and ask yourself, "How do I know that to be true?" Have you been transparent about your thinking and your sourcing? Have you backed up your arguments? Have you been clear when you are pivoting from stating facts to offering your opinion? If not, you are opening yourself up to the critic, and your writing may fail to inform or persuade.

Thinking like a critic can also help you identify potentially off-putting language, particularly if you imagine yourself to be someone different from you—for example, someone from another cultural background or a coworker who is paid substantially less. Adjust your tone or your language to avoid disrespecting or discouraging your reader.

Check Your Facts

You lose credibility fast when you say something that isn't true. Intentionally misleading your reader is the worst offense, but even unintentional errors can damage your reputation, particularly if your reader relies and acts on incorrect information you have provided.

A careful fact-check should be part of your editing process. Examine every statistic, research finding, and quotation and make sure you are reporting it accurately. Go back to the original source—the spreadsheet, the financial report, the research findings, the speech—and make sure you got it right.

If you rely solely on a secondhand account of the facts, you run two risks. The first is that the other person got it wrong, and you're repeating the error. The second is that the other person got the facts right, but you unwittingly introduced a mistake when rephrasing the information. The only way to avoid an error is to look back at the original source and compare it to what you have written.

Sometimes you'll need to rewrite a sentence less precisely after you fact-check it. For example, if you discover you are missing a piece of information, you may need to edit to avoid overstating what you know. This happened to me recently when describing the timing of two contracts. I knew the first was wrapping up this year, and I thought the second was ending the following year. But when I checked my records, I realized I didn't have an end date for the second contract; all I could tell was that it was funded beyond this year. The information wasn't readily available, so I edited my draft to say simply: "One contract will end this year, while the other will continue."

Any time you are quoting or paraphrasing someone else, review your draft to make sure you have reported faithfully what they have said. Don't omit context that changes the meaning, particularly if you are excerpting or using points of ellipsis (. . .) to chop up their statement. And make sure you're attributing the quotation or the concept to the right person. It's an easy mistake to make, because people quote others all the time. But it's embarrassing when you get it wrong. Pity the Postal Service employee who approved a stamp honoring the poet Maya Angelou, featuring not only a portrait of Angelou but also a stirring quote—written by another author. The mistake didn't get caught until the stamp was unveiled to the public, and the media had a field day.

Finally, consider whether to state the source of the information. How much sourcing to do depends on your audience. If you are writing inside a relationship of trust—to close colleagues, for example—you can go light on the sourcing. Your colleagues will know that you use reliable sources and are careful with facts. You should still attribute ideas and insights from others, as appropriate, so you're not stealing their work. If you are citing statistics, source them if your colleagues might wonder where they came from.

You'll have to do more sourcing, however, for a reader who is less trusting, such as a new customer or client. For example, don't just say that your product has the highest reliability rating in the industry; indicate the source of that data. The more skeptical your reader is likely to be, the more complete your citation should be.

Fix Mistakes

You want to be taken seriously when you write on the job. You set that cause back when you make mistakes. Your readers may conclude you're not careful or not capable, particularly if they take care with their own writing. Not all managers, colleagues, or customers will notice your blunders. But why take the risk that they will, and think less of you?

Unfortunately, you can't count on built-in tools like spell-check or auto-correct to catch every mistake. These technologies can even introduce new spelling or grammatical errors when they misunderstand your context or meaning.

Misspellings are a frequent source of error. If you're not confident about your spelling ability, look up a word every time you're not sure how to spell it. Every time. Even if you are a good speller, it's easy to misspell the name of a company, a product, or another person. Make sure to get those right too.

And then there's grammar. Luckily, you don't need to memorize a bunch of rules or terminology to write correctly. But there are a few things you need to get right to avoid looking foolish.

Start by reviewing this paragraph. Can you spot the errors?

> Its difficult to keep "mistakes" out of your writing, even though it effects how people see you. You write a report, your boss says their need to be major improvements before it goes to the client. It would of helped too have followed the principals in this book. Allocate enough time to review your draft— i.e., set aside at least an hour to edit a lengthy document. You loose credibility when your writing appears sloppy. If you have questions about this advice, please contact my editor or I, or any skilled writer's you know.

Here is a corrected version:

> **It's** difficult to keep **mistakes** out of your writing, even though it **affects** how people see you. You write a report, **but** your boss says **there** need to be major improvements before it goes to the client. It would **have** helped **to** have followed the **principles** in this book. Allocate enough time to review your draft— **e.g.**, set aside at least an hour to edit a lengthy document. You **lose** credibility when your writing appears sloppy. If you have questions about this advice, please contact my editor or **me**, or any skilled **writers** you know.

Let's unpack each of these mistakes, so you know how to avoid making them.

Apostrophes. Misusing or omitting an apostrophe is a common grammatical error. Be particularly careful when choosing between it's and its, you're and your, who's and whose, and they're and their (and there). The apostrophe signifies a missing letter: "it **is**," "you **are**," "who **is**," and "they **are**." Without the apostrophe, these words—its, your, whose, and their—instead suggest ownership.

This is confusing because in other contexts, we do use apostrophes to signal possession—for example, the "writer's goals" are the goals of the writer. Nevertheless, when it comes to these little pronouns, it's important to put the apostrophe in its proper place. (Not, "Its important to put the apostrophe in it's proper place.")

Never use an apostrophe to make a word plural. This error runs rampant in holiday greetings—for example, "best wishes from the Brown's" (instead of "the Browns"). But it sneaks into other writing as well, such as the "writer's you know" example above.

Quotation marks. Some of us have a tendency to use quotation marks in our writing even when we're not quoting anything. I'm glad you're reading this book; I'm not glad you're "reading" this book. Quotation marks can also diminish the effect of your words. In the sample paragraph above, the use of quotation marks could leave the reader concerned that the writer doesn't take mistakes seriously, because the writer described them as "mistakes," as if that were someone else's perspective and not the writer's own. Save the quotation marks for times when you're citing material from another source or an unusual expression—or for those rare moments when you do intend to dish out some sarcasm. For example, if I knew my child was playing video games after school instead of finishing a novel for English class, I might text to ask how the "reading" is going.

Commas and semicolons. Commas can make your sentences readable in formal writing like memos and reports, though they are often dispensed with in text messaging and social media. The main error to watch out for is the comma splice, which happens when you string together two separate sentences with a comma. In the example above, the comma-spliced sentence was "You write a report, your boss says there need to be major improvements before it goes to the client." You have three options for remedying a comma splice:

- Break up your sentence, creating two separate sentences. *You write a report. Your boss says there need to be major improvements before it goes to the client.*

- Use a semicolon.
  You write a report; your boss says there need to be major improvements before it goes to the client.

- Insert a simple "but" or "and" after the comma—but not a word like "however," "moreover," or "therefore." Words like "however" must be preceded by a semicolon or used at the start of a new sentence, because they are adverbs and not little connecting words (called conjunctions) like "but" or "and."
  SAY: *You write a report, **but** your boss says there need to be major improvements before it goes to the client.*

  or *You write a report. **However,** your boss says there need to be major improvements before it goes to the client.*

  or *You write a report; **however,** your boss says there need to be major improvements before it goes to the client.*

  BUT NOT: *You write a report, **however** your boss says there need to be major improvements before it goes to the client.*

Commas and semicolons can both be used to separate items in a list, though you should choose semicolons if you are listing items that themselves contain commas. Both of these sentences are correct:

There are three ways to fix a comma splice: break up your sentence, use a semicolon, or insert a "but" or "and."

There are three ways to fix a comma splice: break up your sentence; use a semicolon; or insert a "but" or "and."

There are also a series of tricky word choices you want to make sure to get right. Here are some that frequently trip people up, all of which were illustrated in the error-spotting exercise above.

- **I vs. me (vs. myself).** Does this sentence look right to you? "If you have questions, please contact my editor or I." How about this one? "If you have questions, please contact my editor or myself." They're both grammatically incorrect. The sentence should read: "If you have questions, please contact my editor or **me**." The simple way to choose between I and me is to drop the other person's name. No one would say "please contact I." "Myself" is for situations when the sentence is truly all about you—meaning you are both the subject and the object. For example, "I know myself."

- **Have vs. of.** While it's generally wise to write the way you speak, it can occasionally get you into trouble. In American English, the sentence "It would have helped" sounds exactly like "It would of helped." "Have" is correct; "of" is incorrect.

- **Principal vs. principle.** The word **principal** refers to the leading type of something, the leader of an organization, or a sum of money. For example, the principal reason for reading this book is to improve your writing, which would please your high school principal, who may be paying down the principal on her home mortgage. A **principle** is a core value or idea. It is always a noun, never an adjective. There is no "principle reason" for reading this book.

- **Affect vs. effect.** Affect is ordinarily used as a verb. You seek to **affect** a decision, for example. Effect is typically used as a noun, and means the results of something. The **effect** of reading this book is that you will be a better writer. Used as a verb, it means to make something happen, but it looks funny even if it is technically proper—for example, "she effected change within the company."

- **Lose vs. loose, and to vs. too (vs. two).** We often write one of these words when we mean another. We know the difference; we're just too (not to) careless with our o's.

- **Latin abbreviations.** Written English is sprinkled with handy little abbreviations borrowed from Latin, the language of ancient Rome. If you misuse these terms, anyone who studied Latin in school—and many others—will note the error.

The main mistake we make is to mix up "e.g." and "i.e." They are similar but not identical concepts. The abbreviation **e.g.** means "for example" (in Latin, *exempli gratia*), whereas **i.e.** means "in other words" (in Latin, *id est*, or "that is") and is used for two statements that mean the same thing. The mistaken-ridden paragraph above originally read, "Allocate enough time to review your draft—i.e., set aside at least an hour to edit a lengthy document." Using "i.e." suggests that "enough time" is the same as "at least an hour," which doesn't make sense; reviewing a draft email might only take 5 minutes. What the author meant to say was "*for example*, set aside an hour to edit a lengthy document," so "e.g." is the proper term.

Another tricky Latin abbreviation is **et al.**, which stands for *et alia* (meaning "and the others"). It should always have a period at the end, to signal the missing letters (ia). Similarly, etcetera (in the original Latin, *et cetera*, meaning "and the rest") should always be abbreviated as **etc.**, with a period at the end to signal the missing letters (etera). Et al. and etc. have similar meanings, but et al. is the proper choice when referring to people. For example, if you are citing a report with several authors, you could give the first name and use et al. for the others (e.g., "by Maria Jones et al.").

Finally, much of what we call grammar is a matter of stylistic preference, often influenced by what we were taught in school or by our first boss. If your organization follows a style manual, or if your manager has particular preferences, let those be your guide—even if they seem outdated (or newfangled) to you. But if you're free to make your own choices, here is how I recommend handling some grammatical judgment calls you're likely to encounter.

- **Using "they" as a singular.** An unfortunate thing about the English language is that it lacks an all-purpose pronoun to refer to one person. For a long time, writers just used "he"—as in, "the reader of this book should know what he is getting."

As the role of women in society evolved, "he or she" started to replace "he." But "he or she" is wordy, and especially clumsy when used more than once in a sentence. "The reader of this book should know what he or she is getting, and make sure he or she gets his or her money's worth" sounds awful. Clever writers find ways around the problem—like making the term plural ("readers of this book should know what they are getting"). But coming up with a fix every time can be exhausting.

A growing number of people have argued, persuasively in my view, for using the word "they" to refer to one person. After all, the singular "they" has already crept into our speech, particularly when we use the words "everyone" or "everybody," which are technically singular terms. We nonetheless often say things like "Does everyone know where they are going?" The singular "they" is admittedly hard on the ear of anyone who had the traditional rules drilled into them, but it will get easier with time. So unless your audience will object, it's okay to write "the reader of this book should know what they are getting."

"They" is also the pronoun preferred by many people whose gender identity is nonbinary, because neither "he" nor "she" feels right to them. Even if you don't use the singular "they" in other contexts, you should still respect a coworker or client's pronoun preference and reflect it in your writing.

- **Beginning a sentence with a word like "but" or "and."** Forget what you may have been told about not beginning sentences with conjunctions like "but" or "and." You don't want to overdo it. But in limited doses, it can be effective. See?

- **Ending a sentence or phrase with a preposition.** It makes sense to try to avoid ending a sentence with a preposition, and you certainly shouldn't do it when the word can be dropped altogether—as in "Do you know where the warehouse is **at**?" But sometimes leaving a preposition at the end of a sentence or phrase is the best option. For example, it's fine to write "Do you know what you are looking for?" because it would sound odd to say "Do you know for what you are looking?"

- **The Oxford comma.** When listing three or more items, I find it clearest to insert a comma before the last item. This is sometimes called an Oxford comma or a serial comma. Otherwise you risk the last two items getting blurred together and misunderstood as a description of the first item. For example, you could create some confusion if you wrote, "Appearing at the company picnic will be our CEO, a magician and a Major League Baseball player"—unless your CEO is indeed both a magician and a major leaguer. And if you're listing items that themselves contain commas—using semicolons to separate them—include an "Oxford semicolon" before the last item.

- **Dashes, parentheses, and colons.** I'm a big fan of dashes, as you may have noticed. Used judiciously, they mimic the rhythm of speech and make writing sound more natural. Dashes can be used in pairs—to insert an aside in the middle of a sentence, like this—or at the end of a sentence, to tack on a final point—one you especially want your reader to notice. Parentheses are another option for the midsentence aside, so long as you don't fall into the trap of tucking whole sentences into parentheses, which can be hard for the reader to follow. Colons are an alternative for the end-of-sentence observation, and serve to emphasize what follows. Colons can also introduce a list or a set of bullets.

- **Split infinitives.** It's fine to neatly slide a word between "to" and the rest of a verb. I just did it. Separating your verb can make a sentence more difficult to read, so it's not always the best choice. But avoiding split infinitives at all costs can make your writing more awkward—as in "it's fine neatly to slide a word." Sometimes you get lucky and there's a third way, as there is here, because I could have written "It's fine to slide a word neatly between 'to' and the rest of a verb." Whenever in doubt, read your sentence aloud to decide which order works best.

- **Accent marks.** People from all over the world come to English-speaking countries to live and work, and commerce spans the globe. We should correctly spell the names of the people and companies we interact with, and sometimes those names include accents. It's less important, however, to preserve the accent marks in foreign words that have been adapted into English, because our language does not use accents. So feel free to submit a resume with your cover letter—unless the job posting specifically asked for a résumé, of course. And if the hiring manager is Ms. González, don't send it to Ms. Gonzalez.

Find a Second Pair of Eyes

Having someone else review your writing can be a godsend. If it's a lengthy document, you've probably been living with it for too long and can no longer see the errors or weaknesses. But even a shorter piece can benefit from a second pair of eyes, because you may have made too many assumptions and need someone to spot those gaps or logical leaps for you. Or you may just be prone to typos and need someone to catch them.

The ideal reviewer is someone who represents the audience you're trying to reach. If it's an internal company memo or email, a coworker is fine. If you're writing something aimed at the broader public—like instructions or an op-ed—test it out with someone outside your organization who doesn't have specialized knowledge.

The critical step we often skip when asking a colleague or friend to review our writing is to tell them what to read for. Doing so saves your reviewer time and spares you the awkwardness of getting edits you don't want to take. You have three basic options for the type of feedback to request, and you may wish to ask for any or all of them.

1. **Spelling and grammar.** If you are prone to make mistakes, ask a colleague to spot them for you. If that's all you need, be clear about it by saying, "Could you give this a quick read to check for typos?"

2. **Writing style and clarity.** If you're concerned that your document isn't well written, ask your reviewer to identify places where you're not being clear or where you need to rewrite. You could even explicitly request line edits, if you think they will have the time and be willing to do some of the rewriting for you.

3. **The underlying argument.** If you're confident about your writing but aren't sure how solid your argument is, ask your reviewer if they find the piece persuasive. You're looking for higher-level feedback here—comments rather than edits. Equipped with that guidance, your reviewer may suggest that you de-emphasize one line of argument and add another, or support a point you are making with more data, for example.

When I sent an earlier version of this book manuscript out for review to friends who work in different industries, my cover note said: "I'm mainly looking for feedback on the underlying concepts and the advice I'm imparting, rather than line edits, but if you find errors or awkward passages, that would be great to know too." I got back exactly what I needed—mostly option 3 above, but a helpful smattering of options 1 and 2 as well.

Describe for your reviewer the intended audience, the goal of the piece, and your time frame. If appropriate, say who else has already reviewed the document, or will review it next. And be flexible about how you receive the feedback. Of the sixteen people who reviewed my book manuscript, three chose to provide their feedback in a conversation; five sent back a marked-up document (in three different word-processing programs); and the remaining eight typed up their thoughts in an email. It all worked.

Always thank your reviewer for their feedback, even if you don't agree with it. Most of the time, you won't need to mention the edits you didn't take. If the reviewer is your supervisor, however, or someone else whose approval you need to finalize the document, you will have a choice to make. Either take an edit you don't like, or politely explain why you think the original text (or yet a third variation) would be more effective. Be careful not to let your ego or your emotions cloud your judgment. Often, the best course of action is just to take the edit.

If someone else asks you to look at their work, ask what kind of review they're seeking. It's never wrong to fix typos or egregious grammatical errors. But unless you've been specifically asked for a line edit, resist the temptation to rewrite the piece as you would have written it. There's stylistic variation in writing, and that's a good thing. If we all wrote exactly the same way, we'd be bored to tears. Try reading a bunch of legal documents and you'll see what I mean. You'll also be able to complete your review more quickly if you focus on what your colleague needs from you.

Common Types
of Business Writing

5

Correspondence

Once upon a time, business correspondence consisted entirely of letters. While letters are still used occasionally—to formalize an understanding or make a sales pitch, for example—there has been an explosion in other forms of correspondence. Email plays a central role, but a variety of messaging platforms are now used in many workplaces.

Each type of correspondence has its own style, but there are best practices that apply to them all. This chapter begins with those best practices, then provides additional tips for email, letters, and messaging.

Best Practices across Platforms

First, put the bottom line up front. It aids in comprehension and gets your message across to busy people who triage incoming communications and may not read past the first few lines, at least not initially. State not only the bottom line but also whether any action is needed in response, and if so, by when. Don't manufacture urgency, but if you are working against a hard deadline, be specific about the date and time you need to hear back, rather than saying "soon" or "ASAP."

Second, choose a degree of formality appropriate to your workplace. Email and messaging occupy a gray zone between formal writing and informal speech. Where to land within that zone varies by profession and organizational culture. For example, in some workplaces, text messages without proper punctuation and capitalization are acceptable. In others, they come across as un-professional. Communications with outside vendors or customers will likely need to be written more formally than internal communications. And keep in mind that while typing out a quick message can feel like speaking, a digital record is created every time you communicate—one that can be preserved indefinitely and shared with others, including a much broader audience than you intended, due to the ease of forwarding and screenshotting messages. Pay attention to the words you choose, and pay extra attention when writing about a sensitive topic. Hesitate before writing anything flip, snarky, or sarcastic.

Third, know that when you're writing on the job, the content you create is generally owned and controlled by your employer. Many companies have rules governing the protection of corporate data that they expect employees to follow, and these rules could affect your choice of how to communicate. For example, it might not be appropriate to share confidential financial data or details about a product design on a third-party messaging platform. Emails may be automatically deleted after a period of time, which means you'll have to consider how to preserve critical information. And if you're writing on a topic that could end up the subject of litigation, stick to the facts, so your words are not later misunderstood. Picture yourself in a deposition, listening to your message being read back to you, and ask yourself if you still want to write it.

Fourth, consider how to communicate emotion. You don't want your correspondence to come across as flat, but you also want to be taken seriously. Using emojis or GIFs may make you look silly in some contexts, such as when communicating with someone you don't know well. A best practice is to aim for warmth, which you can accomplish with friendly language and the occasional exclamation point. A former writing student of mine who grew up outside the US once asked, exasperatedly, "What is it with you Americans and all your exclamation points?" Exclamation points are the smiles we put on our writing, and people raised in the US do tend to smile often. That said, using exclamation points after every sentence is like smiling nonstop, which can be awkward. Don't go that far, but do keep in mind that you can unintentionally come across as cold if you don't warm your communications up with a friendly word or punctuation mark. On the other end of the emotional spectrum, if what you're feeling as you write is anger, stop. Wait 24 hours and then resume writing. You'll be surprised at how much you have cooled off, and you'll avoid saying things you'd later regret.

Finally, don't overdo the thank-yous. Expressing gratitude is important when it's meaningful, and researchers have indeed found that people appreciate being thanked at work and wish it would happen more often. But the generic "thanks" in response to a message can be maddening, because it just clogs up inboxes. If you want to thank someone, add a line explaining why you found their contribution useful. Saying "thanks" can also be a way of acknowledging that you received a message or a document, but consider whether it is necessary before doing so. If a colleague is passing something along as an FYI and it's not critical to your work, there's no need to reply. But if an employee sends you a substantial project, acknowledging receipt is appropriate and will be appreciated. Say something specific like "Thanks for sending this. I'll take a look at it and get back to you by the end of the week if I have questions."

Email

A well-structured email gets information to your reader efficiently and makes sure people who skim their messages don't miss the key points. If you can organize and synthesize information clearly in an email, your colleagues and clients will also be more likely to trust that you have a firm grasp on the issue, while a meandering email could lead them to doubt you. Here's how to approach each element of an effective email.

- **Subject lines.** Always use a subject line, and make it brief but informative. Not "FYI" or "News" or "Proposal." The subject line may be all your reader sees when scrolling through their inbox, so you want it to communicate something useful and motivate the reader to read the full message. If your email requires a response, put a question mark at the end of your subject line. For example, "Agenda for staff meeting?" signals that a reply is needed about whether the meeting agenda is ready. I have also found the simple formulation "Quick question about _____?" effective, so long as you don't overuse it with any one person. If you're writing to someone who is notorious for not reading email, you could even put the full question in the subject line ("OK to send slides before 3:00 pitch meeting?"). If you need the recipient to look at a document you are sending, include "for your review" in the subject line, along with a short phrase describing the document (or even "for review by Friday," if you want to emphasize the deadline). Avoid labeling your emails "important" or "urgent," however, since that's in the eye of the beholder. What feels pressing to you may be far down someone else's to-do list.

If you struggle to write a subject line, you may have packed too much into a single email. Try to stick to one topic per email. And if you're on a chain where the topic has evolved, consider starting a new email entirely to avoid confusion, or at least change the subject line. Similarly, if you are forwarding a message—particularly if you're sharing an item from a newsletter or another source—it can help to change the subject line to make clear what the topic is.

- **Salutations.** For a more formal email, begin with "Dear" plus either the person's first name (Dear Beyoncé) or Mr./Ms./Mx. and the last name (Dear Ms. Knowles-Carter), followed by a comma. If you're uncomfortable using just a first name and don't know and can't find out the person's gender, you have a few options. You could write "Hello—" with no name at all or "Dear" and then the full name (Dear Beyoncé

Knowles-Carter), which is becoming more common but may still strike some readers as awkward. Or you could skip the salutation entirely, which may come across as abrupt, but it's not unreasonable given that the person's name is already in the "to" field of the email.

If you know the person well, you can skip the "Dear" and just write the first name (or "Hi" and the first name), followed by a dash or comma. If you're writing to a large group, you may want to start with "Hi everyone," followed by a dash or a comma. When replying to an email, a salutation is not needed, though it may be useful if you want to direct your comments to a particular person on a group message without dropping others off the chain.

- **Opening niceties.** Email feels almost like speaking, which is why our instinct is often to write something friendly before jumping into the business at hand, particularly if we're not in daily communication with the person we're emailing. These opening niceties are appropriate if you know the person, but keep them short and try to personalize them. Don't just write "How are you?" but rather something like "I heard your conference went well—congratulations!" It can even be something about the weather, like "I saw there were blizzards in your area—I hope you've managed to dig out from under all that snow." And then proceed to your bottom line, which you may want to introduce with a phrase like "I'm writing because . . ." or "I wanted to let you know that. . . ."

- **Body of the email.** Your first paragraph should include the opening niceties (if any) and then the bottom line. Never skip the bottom line. Even if you're forwarding something rather than writing an email from scratch, explain why the material you are sharing is worth reading, instead of saying something vague like "This may be of interest." After that first paragraph, and after any succeeding paragraph, insert a blank line to make your email easier to read.

Wherever possible, provide information in bulleted or numbered lists, rather than traditional paragraphs. If you do write paragraphs, keep them short—they should be no more than three sentences, and it's perfectly fine for them to be just one sentence. And don't go on too long, unless your email is performing the function of a report or memo, in which case you should include a summary at the top. You can make selective use of bold print, but don't play around with fonts or color—stick to your system defaults. In some fields, those bursts of creativity can look unprofessional, plus your formatting may get stripped out or modified by the technology on the receiving end. The only time to use color is when crafting an inline reply to a colleague; marking your comments with a standard color like red or blue helps them stand out. Also, if you're attaching a document rather than embedding a link, say so, to prevent it from being overlooked, and give the attachment a file name that will make sense to the reader.

- **Closings.** Quick internal communications may not require any closing line, but most correspondence does. Emails often wrap up with some nicety, such as "Thank you for considering this request," or a reminder of your deadline, such as "I'd appreciate your looking at this by COB Thursday, so we can get it out the door by the end of the week." If there's a specific action you're asking the person to take—which should have appeared up front in your message—it might make sense to repeat that call to action here ("Again, I hope you will . . ."). As for how to sign off, I'm personally a fan of "Thanks in advance—" as a closing line for reasonable requests, though some feel it sounds presumptuous. Two safe bets are your first or full name (perhaps preceded by a dash), or a phrase that uses the word best or regards, such as "Regards," "Best regards," or "All the best" (followed by a comma or dash and then your name on the next line). Closings have evolved over time, however, and will likely continue to do so. For example, "Yours truly" used to be a popular way to end a piece of correspondence, but it sounds stilted today. "Sincerely" is still used, but in more formal communications. Keep an eye on the trends in your profession and decide what makes sense for you.

- **Signature block.** Always put a signature block in external communications to people you don't know well, so it's clear who you are and how to reach you. It can be short—just a line followed by your name, email, and phone number—or you can include additional information like your title, organization, and website. You may wish to create multiple signature files, unless you're confident you want the same information to go out in every email. For example, you might not want everyone you contact to have your phone number. Some people like to put quotations in their signature files, but it's best to avoid those in work emails unless they are uncontroversial, reinforce the brand of your organization, and will be well received by others in your profession.

- **The "to" and "cc" lines.** Filling in the "to" line should be your last step before sending an email. If you complete it earlier, you risk sending an email that you're still in the midst of drafting. If you're replying to a message, consider typing your response in a separate draft window or deleting the names before you start writing, to avoid sending it prematurely.

    As you type in a name, make sure the autofill feature doesn't insert the wrong person's address. And if you're sending to multiple people, list the more senior person first. If you want to cc someone, it may make sense to disclose that in the body of your email, since the cc line is often not readily visible. For example, "My colleague, _____ (cc'd), suggested that I reach out to you."

    Make sure you're not replying all when you mean to reply just to one person, especially when there's a large chain—all of whom may not need to hear that "yes, that time works for me"—or when your reply contains sensitive information.

Using the bcc line is sneaky and can come back to bite you. It's appropriate only if you're (1) emailing a large list of people and putting them all on the bcc line, or (2) replying to a message and stating that you're "moving [name of person] to bcc," which signals that you're dropping someone from a chain to spare them further back-and-forth.

Letters

Letters include just a few essential elements:

- the date;
- the name, organization, and address of the recipient;
- a "Dear _____:" line; and
- your full name at the end (preceded by a closing like "Sincerely").

Beyond that, you have more flexibility than in an email. You can allow some paragraphs to be longer than a few sentences. You don't need to break up your text into bulleted or numbered lists. And you can skip the opening niceties, because letters are more formal and less conversational. It works fine to begin with the bottom line—for example, "I am writing because _____."

If you expect a response, be sure to provide your full contact information, including your email and phone number. It can be either centered at the top in a stationery-style block, placed below your name at the bottom of the page, or included in the final paragraph. For example, your closing line could be "Please contact me with any questions at [email address] or [phone number]."

As for formatting a letter, the simplest approach is to use full block style, where all the text is aligned to the left, no paragraph is indented, and there are blank lines between single-spaced paragraphs.

Messaging

Finally, there is the ever-changing world of messaging. When writing a text or posting on a chat platform, your goal should be to sound professional and appropriate to the medium. Here's how.

- **Keep your message succinct.** When texting, send a series of short messages rather than one long block of text, which might be skimmed through too quickly, resulting in a critical piece of information being overlooked.

- **Consider easing up on the punctuation.** People who have grown up texting and chatting online find it jarring when older people fully punctuate their messages. Periods come across as particularly harsh, even if that's not the intention. For example, "I need to talk to you." (with the period) from a boss sounds like you're about to get reprimanded or fired. More generally, messages are more lightly punctuated than ordinary writing, so you can drop a comma here and there and still sound professional. Similarly, you don't always need to write full sentences, particularly when replying to a message. A quick "on it" or "works for me"—capitalization optional—can be perfectly appropriate.

- **Be careful not to use too much textspeak.** You're likely safe to toss in a "btw" or an "lmk," but think before you use most other abbreviations, especially when communicating with someone of a different generation. And spell out words like "you" (not "u") and "are" (not "r") unless you are communicating with close colleagues and you're confident they won't see it as unprofessional.

- **Add the occasional emoji.** It can be difficult to convey tone in a brief message. Emojis can help, and are even encouraged in some platforms. Just don't overuse them, and make sure you know the meaning of an emoji before you deploy it. GIFs are trickier. They can be entertaining and effective ways to communicate a reaction, but it's best not to use them unless you're communicating with colleagues or customers who know you well and know you take your work seriously. And never use an emoji or GIF that could possibly offend someone. It's unprofessional and unwise.

6

Memos

The typical memo is an internal document written for colleagues or managers. Some memos simply provide an update on a particular matter or a background briefing for an upcoming event, or serve as the mechanism for getting formal approval on an action that doesn't require deliberation. Other memos go further and pitch an idea or tee up a difficult decision that must be made—for example, about a problem that has arisen within the organization or a potential new business opportunity. This chapter focuses on these decision memos, which are more complex and often include a set of options to consider, a discussion of the trade-offs among those options, and a recommended course of action.

Memos can serve as background reading for a meeting, particularly if more than one decision-maker is involved or tough choices need to be made. The best memos are "brilliant and thoughtful and set up the meeting for high-quality discussion," Amazon executive Jeff Bezos once observed.

Writing memos can be an effective way to build your reputation within an organization. One of the best pieces of advice I received as a young congressional aide was to keep coming up with ideas—for an event to host or legislation to introduce—and write them up in short memos. Writing memos keeps you in proactive mode, which can make you a valued team member. Have an idea for improving operations or a new product? Pitch it to your colleagues in a succinct, well-argued memo. You might be surprised how far your idea gets—and how far it gets you.

Memos are also powerful tools for making change. Even if you have firmly established your reputation within your organization, it's a smart strategy to "grab the pen" on a memo outlining a major decision. You demonstrate leadership and wield influence by determining how to frame the issue and argue the case.

A memo should be no more than six pages, to keep your reader focused on the core content. In many workplaces, memos are even shorter—two or three pages. If your draft is too long even after you have used the editing strategies in chapter 4, consider moving some data or other background information to an appendix. And always find a second reader for your memo before you finalize it, to make sure you've explained the issue clearly and laid out your arguments persuasively.

Memo Style

Your tone in a memo should be natural, almost conversational. You can accomplish this while still coming across as professional. A memo that sounds stilted or uses too much jargon will be more difficult to read and therefore less persuasive. Relatedly, memos can be written in the first person, using the word "I" or, in the case of a coauthored memo, "we." Address your audience as "you."

An internal memo should be written candidly. Memos should never withhold relevant information or alternative viewpoints, even if they weaken your case. The best decisions are made with eyes wide open. Whatever risk you're downplaying will likely come out in the end anyway in a follow-up discussion, or worse, when implementing your recommended course of action. The only time to keep information out of a memo is when it is sensitive or confidential and you fear the document could leak to a competitor or the media.

Memo Structure

A short briefing memo does not need much structure, other than a header and some limited formatting—such as bulleted lists or bold print—to help the reader navigate the text. A decision memo, however, should include five elements:

1. a **header** (stating the author's name, the recipient's name, the subject, and the date);

2. a **short summary** at the top (typically one paragraph);

3. a brief **background** section;

4. a **lengthier analysis section** that uses informative subheadings to guide the reader through the discussion; and

5. a **recommendation** on how to proceed, if appropriate.

This structure has several advantages. It helps the reader absorb the information and arguments you are presenting, rather than getting distracted by trying to figure out the purpose of the memo or follow your train of thought. Furthermore, like it or not, some readers skim through memos instead of reviewing them carefully, whether for lack of time or lack of interest. A skimmer can scan through your memo and grasp the core takeaways if you have included a summary paragraph at the top and clear headings and subheadings. A well-structured memo also can serve as a helpful reference document, allowing someone who has read it once to look back at it and easily extract relevant information.

The first step in structuring your memo is to put the bottom line up front. Each memo should begin with a short paragraph stating the purpose and summarizing the conclusions reached. If the memo recommends a course of action, that should be mentioned in this first paragraph as well.

The next section, which is the background, should be short—no more than three paragraphs. It should be a table setter for the analysis and recommendation that follow, and contain only enough background context to understand the rest of the memo. Weave any other critical information into the analysis section as supporting evidence.

Keep in mind that you may possess much more information than you can include in the background section. That's to be expected, because you are likely the in-house expert on this particular topic. Your job is to winnow down what you have learned into what your colleagues need to know. Writing a memo is not a "show what you know" exercise; it's a "tell me what I need to know" exercise. Always keep your audience at the front of your mind.

The background section might, for example, include some history on the issue—why it's of interest, or what has been tried in the past. Or if it's a data-driven memo, you might explain how you approached the analysis you will be presenting. It's fine to include information your reader may already know if you would otherwise risk confusion. If you're worried about insulting your reader's intelligence, you can always preface statements with an "as you may recall" or "as you may know."

The analysis section is the heart of the memo. It is also the most free-form element. Your task is to figure out the key points you want to make, turn them into succinct subheadings, and structure your discussion around them. If you've prepared a bullet outline, it will help you assemble the analysis section. Aim for three subheadings, which is a manageable number of points for the reader to take in, though more (or fewer) are acceptable. Use informative subheadings that state conclusions, rather than listing topics. For example, a subheading should say "Adding a New Product Line Would Be Costly" instead of "The Costs and Benefits of Adding a New Product Line."

Consider using bullets and other formatting tools in your analysis section. Bullets and numbered lists are particularly helpful when laying out a set of research findings or concepts that go together. Like data visualizations, they also break up the text and make it easier to read. However, excessive bulleting will make your memo disjointed.

The final section states your recommended course of action. Your recommendation may be apparent by the time the reader gets through your analysis, but you should still be clear about what needs to happen to address the issue raised in your memo. Be as specific as possible about what should be done by whom in what time frame, and explain your thinking. If you want your memo to get results, your reader needs to come away with a solid understanding of the issue and the specific action steps you recommend.

How to Be Persuasive in a Memo

First and foremost, back up your claims. Your memo will not be persuasive if it consists merely of a series of assertions. Explain your reasoning and support your arguments with the best available evidence.

You should also anticipate and address counterarguments. Be up front about any competing viewpoints or the limitations of the evidence you are presenting. Explain why you nonetheless reach your conclusions, and be honest about how confident you feel about the recommendation you are putting forward and any potential downsides. Imagine a skeptic sitting on your shoulder as you write. What would it take to convince that person you've done a fair job of analyzing the issue? Demonstrating that you've thought through all the angles also gives you credibility with your audience.

Consider the full range of options for how to address the issue raised in your memo before settling on a recommendation, and mention any alternative approaches you or your reader might see as reasonable. You can collect this discussion under a single subheading at the end of the analysis section, or weave it in along the way.

Finally, get your facts straight. One of the quickest ways to lose credibility with your colleagues is to play fast and loose with the truth, or even just to be sloppy. A serious error in your memo not only makes you look bad; it also risks embarrassing others who rely on what you have told them. It's fine to include a piece of information you're not certain is accurate, so long as you provide a disclaimer. For example, you could say "the data appear to indicate _____, though _____," or "_____ is rumored to be _____." If you simply don't have a crucial piece of information, that's okay too. Just say "I would be more confident in this recommendation if we knew _____. Unfortunately, that information is not available, and we need to make a decision."

Memo Format

The line spacing in a memo should be above 1 but no greater than 1.5, with blank lines between paragraphs. White space on the page gives the reader's eyes a momentary rest, which is helpful both in print and on a screen. Blank lines also signal that a new thought is coming, by creating a break before the next paragraph.

Always number your pages. Numbered pages are a convenience to the reader and make it easy to refer to a particular part of the document in a follow-up discussion.

Avoid playing with the margins or font size if you possibly can. If your memo is too long, go back and edit it again, or move some material to an appendix. Reducing margins to less than 1 inch or dropping below the standard 12-point font size will make your memo less readable.

Try not to use footnotes. Footnotes are distracting, because they send the reader up and down a page and disrupt the flow of your narrative. Depending on the culture of your organization, however, you may need to use footnotes, endnotes, or hyperlinks to provide citations for sources you relied on in your analysis. Be sure to provide in any footnotes or endnotes only the information necessary to track down the source, and not additional commentary.

Even in a footnote-free memo, if you are relying on someone else's findings, you should mention the source of the information. You can do this briefly in the body of the memo by ending your sentence with a phrase like "according to a study published last year in _____" or "as research by our marketing department has shown."

Memo formats vary across organizations, though they have a similar look. The template provided here is adapted from the format used for decision memos in the White House.

You'll see a header followed by a "bottom line up front" paragraph stating the purpose and conclusions reached, and then the body of the memo, divided into three parts: background, analysis, and recommendation.

For the header, if you are sending the memo to more than one person, list the names on the "to" line in alphabetical order—though a very senior person, like a CEO, should always come first. Provide your title as well as your name on the "from" line if the recipient might not know exactly who you are.

To: Full name of recipient

From: Your full name

Subject: Something short and direct, like How to
           Write a Memo

Date: Month Day, Year (for example, January 1, 2022)

This memo discusses/analyzes/presents/provides an update on
_____, *if appropriate, add:* in response to your request for
_____. It concludes/explains that [*list your main points here,
borrowing language from the subheadings below*]. It recommends
that [*summarize your recommendation*].

BACKGROUND
[1–3 paragraphs providing context for your reader]

ANALYSIS

*Subheading 1 [For example: Memos Should Contain
Informative Subheadings]*
[1–5 paragraphs backing up this claim]

Subheading 2
[1–5 paragraphs backing up this claim]

Subheading 3
[1–5 paragraphs backing up this claim]

RECOMMENDATION
[Describe in 1–3 paragraphs your recommended course of action,
including any specific steps that must be taken.]

7

Proposals, Plans, and Reports

There are certain documents that lack consistent names across organizations. One company's white paper is another's strategic plan. But the core content usually falls in one of three categories:

- a proposal (explaining what you would like to do),
- a plan (explaining how you will do it), or
- a report (explaining what you did or where things stand).

Here's how to approach each of these three types of writing, though keep in mind that you may end up combining them. For example, a proposal could also include a detailed plan or a report on past activities.

Proposals

To write a successful proposal, figure out what the reader cares about and expects. If you're writing in response to a request for proposal (RFP), that's your bible. Comb through it to determine what precise information is requested and in what order and level of detail. This is not a time for experimenting. Your writing can be lively, but unless your content matches what's listed in the RFP, your proposal could end up getting rejected out of hand.

If you don't have an RFP as your guide, you can still engage in audience analysis before you begin writing. Think through how the products or services you're offering will help meet the reader's needs or goals, and make sure that comes through clearly throughout the proposal.

A proposal should explain to the reader

- **who you are**,
- **why you're qualified** to provide the service you are offering,
- **what you are offering** (including the timing and budget, if appropriate), and
- **how they will benefit**.

As for structure and format, look for clues in the RFP if you have one. If you don't, stick to the best practices that apply to other documents, including stating the bottom line up front and using headings, bullets, bold print, and other formatting tools to make your document easy to read. To project confidence, say what you "will" do, rather than what you "would" or "could" do. And if your proposal is for internal use—for example, making the case for a change in a business process—consider presenting your proposal in problem-solution form.

Plans

A plan describes a course of action. It tells the reader who is going to do what, when, and why. While there are many ways to structure and format a plan, it should always contain these elements, though you may label them differently:

- **objective** (what you are trying to accomplish)
- **strategy and tactics** (how you will accomplish it)
- **timeline** (what will happen when)
- **staffing** (who will be responsible for what tasks)
- **metrics** (how to assess whether you have succeeded)

Don't be overly optimistic in your plan. It can undermine your credibility or, if your plan is followed, lead to failure. Some organizations go a step further in their written plans and build in a risk analysis, which is a discussion of how the plan could go wrong and strategies for preventing or responding to those contingencies.

Reports

A report describes something that has happened in the past, or the current state of an ongoing project or activity. It is not designed to elicit a response, though the reader may choose to act on the findings. Memos (covered in chapter 6) are sometimes used to deliver brief reports, but anything longer than six pages should be written as a stand-alone report.

The main elements of a report are

- a **title page** (with the name of the report, its authors, and their institutional affiliations, as well as the date);

- a **table of contents**;

- an **executive summary** (1–3 pages);

- the **body of the report**, which presents the findings and analysis;

- **recommendations** (if appropriate to the topic);

- **methodology** (if appropriate to the topic); and

- **endnotes** (for any citations in the text).

The bulk of the report is in the body. You can include an introduction within the body of the report, to provide basic context for what follows, but avoid repeating too much of what is in the executive summary. A paragraph or two should suffice. There's no need to write a conclusion; if you have next steps that you propose taking, they belong in the recommendations section.

Particularly if you're writing a long report, it's critical to use formatting to make the content more digestible. Consider laying the text out in columns, and don't be afraid to leave blank space, including when you begin a new section or chapter. To break up the narrative, add pull quotes, callout boxes, and data visualizations.

If different people have written sections of the report, make sure you designate one person to review and edit the final document. Conforming changes will likely be needed in the style, tone, formatting, and even the sentence and paragraph structure.

8

Critical Feedback

To be effective at your job, you must be able to communicate when something isn't working and needs to be fixed. Sometimes that's best done in person, where tone of voice and facial expressions can help, but critical feedback is often provided in writing. Knowing how to write criticism well can not only improve your work relationships but also get you better results.

A common form of critical feedback is the performance review, and this chapter provides specific suggestions for how to approach those documents. But it begins with some more broadly applicable advice about how to respond to anything from a client email proposing a bad idea to a colleague's memo containing flawed analysis.

Getting Heard

None of us like to be criticized. Our instinct is to defend ourselves, rather than open our minds to the possibility that the other person might be right. So how can you make sure your feedback is heard and acted upon?

Thoughtfully structuring your feedback helps. This is one of the few areas where bottom line up front isn't the wisest approach. Begin instead on a neutral or positive note rather than launching into the substance of your criticism right away. For example, you could start with a point of agreement to establish some common ground. It could be something as simple as "This is a difficult problem to solve" or "We all want to deliver an excellent product." Or you could go a step further and use the criticism sandwich. I am a fan of this approach, though it has its detractors. The idea is to "sandwich" the criticism between more positive comments that start and end the communication. For example, "This contains a number of creative ideas. I'm concerned they won't be workable given our financial constraints and the personnel we have available for this project. But let's keep thinking together about how we might accomplish our objectives." Critics say they see right through the sandwich and it therefore defeats the purpose. I maintain that even if you see through it, the sandwich makes the criticism easier to swallow.

You should also be as specific as possible and provide a path forward. If you don't like an idea, suggest an alternative. If you don't like how something is written, show how you would rewrite a paragraph or restructure the document. It takes more time and effort on your part, but it's more likely to move the ball forward.

Above all, be fair in your criticism, and don't let negative emotions slip into your words. You won't get far if what you've written comes across as an attack on the person, instead of a well-considered reaction to an idea.

Performance Reviews

The purpose of a performance review is to help an employee improve. To be credible, it has to be fair. To be actionable, it has to be specific. Start by looking back at the employee's previous review. What goals and standards were laid out, and how did you evaluate whether they were met? Be consistent and identify achievements and strengths the employee can build on, rather than lingering on weaknesses they're unlikely to overcome.

Consider asking employees to write the first draft, sometimes called a self-assessment or self-evaluation. Encourage them to be as concrete as possible, both in reflecting back on their experiences and in setting goals they expect to be held accountable for in future reviews.

You may wish to solicit input from their peers as well, since they often interact more with each other than with supervisors and are therefore in a position to bring useful information to light. Some people also feel more comfortable praising a coworker than bragging about themselves. One caution: This approach only works in a well-functioning workplace, where biases or personal conflicts don't cloud the judgment of the people providing feedback.

When it comes time for you to write the final review, you can structure your feedback in a criticism sandwich or by starting on a point of agreement, as noted above. If you're inclined to go for the sandwich, keep in mind that there is always something positive you can say, even about a low performer, whether it's about the approach they take or how they support their coworkers. For example, you might say "_____ has worked hard this year. The results have been mixed, and our clients have not always been satisfied. But lessons learned from those experiences may provide a foundation to build on in the future." Note that the praise is limited (hard work), while the criticism is substantial (mixed results and dissatisfied clients). But it's not so overwhelmingly negative that it offers no path forward.

If you are writing a performance review for someone who is performing so poorly that their job is in jeopardy, make sure you understand your organization's HR policies and practices. You are creating a record that could ultimately be part of a legal dispute, so be fair and choose your words carefully.

9

Resumes and Cover Letters

A well-crafted resume and cover letter can open doors that might otherwise have remained closed. This is particularly true in the early stages of your career, when a well-written letter can help you stand out from the crowd. But no matter how experienced you are, it's always worth putting in the time to make sure your resume and cover letter make the best possible case for hiring you.

This chapter explains how to design a resume and write an effective cover letter. It begins by emphasizing the importance of analyzing your audience.

Remember: It's Not about You

You should always consider your audience when you get started on any piece of writing. This can feel counterintuitive when it comes to resumes and cover letters, because we see them as opportunities to talk about ourselves. Here's the problem with that approach. You could succeed in persuading the reader that you're terrific and still not get an interview, because the reader might conclude that you are great—just not for this job. You need to convince the reader that you're the right person for *this particular job at this particular organization.*

Here's a simple test. Do you use the same cover letter every time you apply for a job? If so, you aren't tailoring the letter enough to your audience. Even resumes sometimes need to be modified. The facts can't change, but you can emphasize some experiences or responsibilities over others. You'll likely need multiple versions of your resume if you're searching in a few different fields. Even if you're staying in the same field, you may need to make modest tweaks to ensure all the required elements in a particular job listing appear on your resume.

Keep in mind that your first audience might be a computer. Many large employers use artificial intelligence technologies to screen applicants, searching for keywords that match the skills, experience, and education requirements listed in the job posting.

Resumes

A resume is a simple document listing your contact information, work experience, educational background, and—if appropriate for your profession—skills. Here are tips for creating an effective resume, most of which also apply to writing an online professional profile. Employers often use these profiles to recruit or assess potential candidates, so you want them to be as well crafted as your resume.

- **Limit your resume to one page, if possible.** If you are early in your career, there is no need for a resume longer than a page. It just makes it harder to find the most relevant information, and risks it being overlooked. To fit everything on one page, consider what matters for the jobs you're seeking. If you have a college degree, there's no need to mention high school. Include a personal interest or activity only if it plays an important role in your life or if you see a connection to the job. For example, volunteer work may be relevant when seeking employment with a charitable organization. Be specific enough to catch the attention of a recruiter or interviewer. For example, you could mention participating in a local soccer league, but don't bother to list "working out" among your interests. There's no need to put an objective or summary at the top unless you're changing job types and want to make clear what kind of position you're seeking. "References available upon request" should be obvious, so save yourself that line too.

If you are mid- or late career and a one-page resume won't do justice to what you have to offer, consider organizing your professional experience thematically, rather than in a single reverse-chronological list. My own two-page resume has four categories: current employment (listing the consulting, teaching, and writing work I do now), executive branch experience, legislative branch experience, and nonprofit experience. It's more intuitive and navigable than a lengthy chronology.

- **Choose a style that suits your audience.** In general, resumes should have a simple, consistent look, to make it easy for the reader (which could be a computer) to extract the relevant information. That means selecting a commonly used font, listing accomplishments in bullets, and structuring your headings and subheadings with tools like bold, italics, and underlining. However, if you work in a creative field, the expectations may be different. Consistency is still important, but it may be appropriate to use an unusual font, a more design-forward layout, or even an image. Take your cues from how others in your profession format their resumes.

- **Avoid insider jargon.** Explain past job responsibilities using language that will be understandable to people outside your organization and even outside your field, if you're conducting a broader search.

- **Use action-oriented verbs.** Your resume should present you in an active role, so the reader can picture you accomplishing things, instead of passively taking direction from others. You can do this by selecting strong, action-oriented verbs, then carefully filling in the detail to avoid taking credit for someone else's work. Wherever possible, use the same verbs that are in the job listing.

STRONG RESUME VERBS:

built
championed
conducted

coordinated
created
developed
directed
engaged
guided
launched
led
managed
presented
supervised
trained

WEAK RESUME VERBS AND PHRASES:

assisted
helped
participated
responsible for
served
supported
worked

You will likely have some weak verbs on your resume, because there will be situations where you can't use a stronger verb. That's fine, and appropriate. Just look for opportunities to take credit. For example, identify projects you "created" or "led," even if they were small ones. They demonstrate leadership and initiative, which are more compelling to a prospective employer than a detailed accounting of your daily responsibilities. To keep yourself honest, imagine showing your resume to someone who worked with you. Would you be worried about their reaction? If so, you need to dial back the credit-taking.

Cover Letters

The biggest mistake you can make when writing a cover letter is to summarize your resume. That duplicates effort, because the information is already contained in the resume. More importantly, it misses the opportunity to make a targeted pitch for why this employer should hire you.

An effective cover letter explains how you can help carry out an organization's mission. The narrative has to be driven by the employer's needs, not the highlights of your resume or your personal ambitions. As a result, you may need to emphasize certain aspects of your background in your cover letter and skip over others entirely. You want the reader's reaction to be "Wow, this person is just what we're looking for," not "I don't know why this person is applying for this job."

How do you know what the employer is looking for? Read the job posting carefully, and review their website and social media accounts to learn how they talk about themselves. Make sure you understand, before you start writing, what they do and what they need, so you can use that knowledge to frame your communications and draw specific connections to your background and experiences. But put it in your own words. If you borrow too much language directly from the employer, they'll spot it right away, and you'll come across like a robot.

As for length, stick to one page. If you're making a targeted, compelling pitch, you shouldn't need more than a single page.

Here's an example of how to structure an effective cover letter.

Dear [name or "hiring manager"],

I am writing to express interest in the position of _____
_____ at _____ [name of organization]. *If appropriate, add*: I learned of this position from [name of connection], who suggested that I apply. *Say something about the value the organization creates—for example,* "I am attracted to Company X because of its reputation for providing high-quality services to its clients" *or* "Nonprofit Y does such important work addressing the needs of our community"—*but be as specific as possible, to show that you understand what the organization does and how it distinguishes itself from others*. I would be excited to join your team and contribute

_____ [describe what you offer—for example, "my data analysis skills" or "my sales experience"] to help carry out your mission.

I understand that you are seeking _____ [describe a skill or qualification in the job posting]. I have experience _____ [describe how you demonstrated those qualities or delivered a result similar to what they are seeking, in a professional or educational setting].

Second paragraph with a different example of what they are seeking and how you could meet their needs.

Optional third paragraph with yet another example.

The enclosed resume details my professional experience and educational background. I can be reached at [email] or [phone], and look forward to hearing from you.

Sincerely,
[your full name]

Make sure your cover letters and resumes are error-free. Your boss or a client might forgive the occasional typo or misspelling in your memos or correspondence. A hiring manager is far less likely to forgive an error in a cover letter or resume. It suggests that you are careless, which is not a sought-after quality in the job market. If you don't trust yourself to catch all your errors, ask an eagle-eyed friend or colleague to review what you've written before you submit it.

Numbers and Visuals

10

Writing about Numbers

When writing about numbers, you want your reader to easily understand the data you're using and any conclusions you draw. To accomplish this, you may literally need to do the math. It's not enough to spill numbers onto the page; tell your reader what the relationship is between them.

After you've written a sentence, consider whether the story you're trying to tell is immediately apparent or whether the reader has to do math in their head to figure it out. That mental arithmetic disrupts the flow of your writing; plus some people find it challenging, and no one appreciates having to do it. For example, if annual sales increased from $450,000 to $850,000, say that they "nearly doubled." If the raw data are important or useful to the reader, couple them with an explanatory narrative. Say "Sales nearly doubled, rising from $450,000 to $850,000."

Now that you know to "do the math," here are additional strategies for writing about numbers.

Provide Context

If you're telling a story with numbers, provide sufficient context for your reader to understand the significance. For example, when describing a change over time, give the start and end dates. Don't just say "our sales were up by $1 million in March"; explain what time periods you're comparing. It could be that sales this March were $1 million higher than in February, or that sales in March were $1 million higher than in the previous March. Those are different statements, and readers may wish to know which you mean.

If you're reporting on market research or survey data, explain the relevance of a finding, particularly in an internal communication where you want to be transparent. Was a survey question asked in an open-ended manner, or was a selection made from a menu of options? If there was a menu, what else was on it? For example, if you've written that most customers said price was an "important" consideration in choosing among products, consider the other options on the survey. If "very important" and "extremely important" were also listed but few people selected them, disclose that information too. It paints a more complete picture for your reader of how price-sensitive your customers are (or aren't).

Be Careful with Averages

Averages are so tempting, because they provide one tidy number. The question to ask yourself is whether the average tells the full story. A good way to decide is by looking at the distribution that the average represents. If the numbers in the distribution are close to one another, using an average is fine. If they're spread far apart, an average may do more harm than good.

For example, it could make sense to describe a community where residents' incomes range from $50,000 to $70,000 as having an average income of $60,000. But if half of residents earned less than $50,000 while the other half pulled down over $1 million, it would be misleading to say the average income is approximately $500,000. No one who lives there is making that amount, yet you've left your reader picturing someone who is, and potentially making ill-advised decisions as a result.

Avoid Percentage Confusion

Percentages are wonderful for describing a situation at a point in time. A statement like "90% of customers are satisfied with the service they receive at our company" is straightforward. The trouble begins when we use percentages to describe a change over time or to make another comparison, because it requires the reader to do or understand math. For example, a 100% increase means something has doubled, while a 200% increase means it has tripled. That is not common knowledge.

Similarly, readers are often tripped up by the difference between percentages and percentage points. We react very differently if we are told the risk of getting cancer is 50% higher if we engage in a certain activity than if we are told the risk is one percentage point higher. Yet both could be true, if the risk rises from 2% to 3%. The 50% sounds terrifying, and some people may even think it means that there is a 50% risk of getting cancer. The one percentage point increase sounds like a potentially acceptable risk. Think about the impression you want to give your reader.

Compare Apples to Apples

Even journalists sometimes make the mistake of mixing apples and oranges. I once read a media report explaining that in Kenya, "there are around 40 cardiologists for the entire population of 48 million people," while in the US "there is one cardiologist for every 13,000 people." It's difficult to compare those two statements, unless you do some further calculations of your own. Perhaps the writer was compelled by the statistic that there are only 40 cardiologists in all of Kenya, and indeed it is striking. But once the comparison with the US is introduced, the numbers get confusing. A better way to present this narrative would be to say: "There are only 40 cardiologists in all of Kenya. That's 1 for every 1.2 million people, compared to 1 for every 13,000 in the US."

Avoid False Precision

Our brains are wired to assign unnecessary weight to a number when it is stated precisely, such as with a string of decimals. When you're providing an estimate or an illustrative number, it's best to round it to avoid conveying a false sense of precision. Say that it will cost your company $2 million to implement a new technology, not $1,980,730—even if that's the figure you estimated in a spreadsheet. If you have a precise figure but it is not necessary to the argument or explanation you are providing, go ahead and round it to make it easier for your reader to absorb. Say that a company employs approximately 4500 people, even if you have point-in-time data showing the figure is 4487. That said, it's appropriate to give a precise number when you have one and it's meaningful. If a stock is trading at $157.75, you wouldn't say it's trading at $160.

Choose Relatable Units

Whenever possible, express numbers in terms your reader can visualize or imagine. If you're communicating with the public, keep in mind that most people can't get their heads around millions or billions, and percentage changes sound abstract. But talking about dollars per person gets their attention. For example, one of the most powerful criticisms of the pharmaceutical industry's role in the opioid epidemic was the revelation that companies shipped hundreds of pills per resident to some counties, a more relatable statistic than the millions of pills per county.

Use Symbols

Symbols are not only acceptable but helpful in business writing. There's no reason to write out "fifty percent" when 50% does the job so neatly. Similarly, say $1000 instead of "one thousand dollars" or "$10 million" instead of "ten million dollars." The symbol versions take up less space and stand out more, especially when skimming or rereading a document.

11

Data Visualizations

Data visualizations can enhance many types of writing. Charts and graphs are often the centerpieces of slide decks and reports, and appear frequently in memos and proposals as well. And they are a huge asset in social media.

The power of a good visual is that it helps people absorb and retain information. Including a visual in a written document can also make it more persuasive. Studies have found that consumers are more likely to believe a product is effective if a description of the product is accompanied by a graph, even if the graph provides no additional information.

The best visualizations are often the simplest ones. The more quickly your audience is able to understand your visualization, the less it will disrupt your flow. The goal should be to convey a single idea, which your reader should be able to grasp without thinking too hard or doing math.

This chapter explains how to design the basic visuals generated by standard office software, such as bar graphs, line graphs, pie charts, and tables. There are many other kinds of data visualizations to explore, including word clouds, waffle charts (grids with some of the small boxes filled in), dot plots (where dots take the place of bars or lines), and maps. Use traditional maps with caution, however, because the uneven geographic distribution of human populations can distort the visual effect. In the US, for example, some of the largest states have the fewest people (think of Alaska or Montana). To show the footprint of a company or the prevalence of a problem, add appropriately scaled dots on top of a state or country, rather than simply coloring it in. Or use a carto-gram, which is a map that has been resized to avoid geographic distortions.

How do you create streamlined, compelling data visualizations? Let's start by considering this bar graph, which was automatically generated by spreadsheet software.

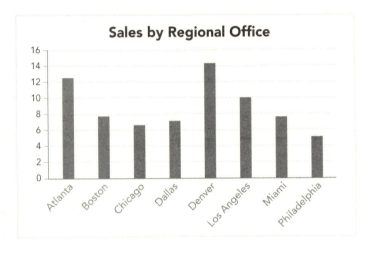

Here is a step-by-step approach to improving a simple visual like this.

Step 1: Arrange your data in a logical pattern. A bar graph is easier to read if the bars are ordered by height (or length, for a hori-zontal bar graph). This allows the audience to quickly judge rela-tive sizes and draw conclusions, which is difficult to do with a graph that looks like the one above. You can't do this for a bar or line graph that shows a time series, but many graphs lend themselves to reordering. Similarly, a pie chart is easier to read if the largest piece (which should begin at the 12 o'clock position) is adjacent to the second-largest piece, and so on.

Step 2: Draw the reader's eye to the key elements of your visual. You can do this by adding an arrow or a circle, or by using shading, a heavier line, or a different color. Color sometimes has the added advantage of conveying meaning, and can give the reader an instant snapshot of the situation. For example, if you are presenting a table of numbers, you can color negative indicators red, positive indicators green, and any neutral or in-between indicators yellow. Just make sure your visual can still be understood without the help of the red-green distinctions, since a significant share of the population has some degree of color blindness.

Step 3: Provide horizontal labels and avoid legends. Whenever possible, apply labels directly to the relevant elements of your graphic—above a bar, on a pie slice, adjacent to a line, or on an axis. Orient the text horizontally, so readers don't have to tilt their heads. And avoid legends if you possibly can. They create an undesirable two-step interpretive process, which you can prevent by applying labels directly to your data elements instead. The spreadsheet software didn't create a legend for this graph, but they are often automatically generated for line graphs and pie charts.

Step 4: Strip out unnecessary elements, like extraneous gridlines. Look at your data visualization and ask yourself if there are any elements you can remove, to simplify the image without taking away necessary content. Gridlines are a likely candidate, particularly if you have already labeled each data point, or if your purpose is to demonstrate a trend rather than to convey specific numbers.

Step 5: Provide a helpful title. Your data visualization shouldn't be an intelligence test. Crafting an informative title tells your reader what the point is. Having to write a title also ensures you know the answer to that question yourself. If you are struggling to write a good title, you may have dumped data into a visualization without thinking enough about why you want your audience to see it.

Here's what our bar graph looks like after making those five simple improvements, all of which can be accomplished using basic spreadsheet software. If you have access to more sophisticated tools, even more possibilities open up, but you can get far even without design software or skills.

The data is now arranged in a logical pattern (step one), from highest to lowest sales. It also now appears as horizontal bars, rather than vertical bars, to reinforce the idea that the Denver office is "on top," as we might say in describing the data. For emphasis, the Denver bar is now shaded darker than the others (step two). If this were a color chart, you could instead make the Denver bar green—which is a positive, "go" color that also symbolizes money in the US—while leaving the other bars in the more neutral gray. If the purpose of the graph were to highlight the performance of a different office, we could have chosen to darken or color in that bar instead. The graph now has horizontal labels (step three). Each bar now has a data label, and there is a horizontal line of text explaining that the figures are sales in millions of dollars. The names of the regional offices are also easier to read, because they are no longer tilted. The gridlines are gone, because the data labels made them superfluous (step four). For this particular visualization, I went further and eliminated one axis line altogether, since the data labels provide the necessary information. Finally, the title now conveys the takeaway message (step five), which is that Denver has the most sales.

Making these simple changes takes only a few minutes, once you get the hang of it. It saves your audience time and, more importantly, leads to a visual that is more likely to inform and stick with them.

12

Slide Decks

Slide decks have become nearly ubiquitous in today's workplace. In many business environments, they are expected at most meetings and nearly all presentations, whether in person or online. Miss the meeting? No worries—just "send me the slides," we say.

The wonderful thing about slide decks is that they provide an easy way to use visuals to enhance a conversation and reduce the need for note-taking. The terrible thing about slide decks is that they can turn what would have been a dynamic presentation into a monotonous parade of "next slide," which drains the energy from any room. A slide deck should not be the text of a report or memo converted to lengthy bullets, yet that's how many are created.

This chapter guides you through the process of assembling an effective slide deck. It begins with advice on slide design, then discusses how to structure your deck, and concludes with tips on how to present it.

Before you even open your presentation software, however, figure out what you want to say. The mechanical act of compiling a slide deck risks substituting for strategic thinking. If you create your slides before you sketch out an outline or talking points, you'll end up saying things like "now this slide shows that. . . ." That's hardly an engaging presentation strategy. (For advice on how to put together an effective set of remarks, see chapter 16.)

Slide Design

How your slides should look depends on how you plan to use them, as well as on the expectations and standards in your industry.

- If your slides are being **displayed on a screen while you speak,** keep them streamlined, so the audience isn't struggling to interpret the slides and listen to you at the same time. Each slide should serve as a backdrop, and include no more than a short phrase, simple data visualization, or compelling image that reinforces the point you are making. In addition to the cognitive dissonance that denser slides can create, your audience may also struggle to read them if the elements are too small, whether you're appearing in person or virtually.

- If your slides are being **used in a meeting** where your audience is reading a hard copy or scrolling through the deck on a personal screen, you have more leeway to put additional words or more complex visuals on each slide. But be careful not to overdo it; you could create the same cognitive dissonance effect, because your audience will still be both listening and reading.

- If your slides are a "**leave-behind**" and are therefore expected to be content-rich, open with a streamlined set of slides and provide an appendix with additional material, rather than making the slides in your core presentation too dense.

As for industry expectations, they can vary greatly, so find out what your audience is likely to want. For example, a pitch deck prepared for a venture capital firm is typically ten slides or fewer, with a premium placed on a strong narrative and compelling visuals. But in some other professional settings, decks are expected to be longer, and a thin deck may be frowned upon.

No matter what the audience or the industry expectations, here are some basic rules to follow in designing your slides to make them audience-friendly.

- **Use a consistent format.** Your slides should all have the same look, fonts (no more than two per deck), and color palette (no more than three per deck). Templates built into presentation software make this easy. Your organization may even have its own templates. Select or create your own template, and resist the temptation to deviate from it unless you have a knack for design. You'll end up with slides that look less professional. If you're using a chart or graph from another source, re-create it if you can, so the look of your slides remains consistent.

- **Craft informative titles.** Each slide should convey no more than one core message. A title that communicates that message helps the audience quickly grasp the point of a data visualization or a block of text, so they aren't tuning you out while they try to figure it out for themselves. And just as with the headings in a memo or report, your audience should be able to skim through the titles on your slides and get the gist of your presentation.

- **Limit your use of text-only slides**. Slide decks are a visual medium. If you're sharing numbers, try to present them in a data visualization rather than through text. If you do need to put words on some slides, intersperse those slides with a data visualization or another image, like a photograph. Wherever possible, write a simple phrase or sentence rather than a string of bullet points.

  If you do use bullet points, limit yourself to three, make sure they use parallel grammatical structure (so they're all either complete sentences or fragments), and never use sub-bullets. If you get to that point, you likely have far too much text on your slides, and you need to pare it back or break up the slide.

  Consider using graphic icons that symbolize your content instead of plain dots for your bullets. These monochrome icons are available online at low cost, and they're more professional looking than clip art, which you should generally avoid. There are other ways to visually enhance a text slide— for example, if you are quoting a testimonial from a customer or a product review from the media, you could put your content in a text bubble (sometimes called a speech balloon) along with the organization's logo. Avoid flowcharts or diagrams, however, unless you are describing sequential steps in a process. Images like hub-and-spoke diagrams may look appealing at first glance, but they're more likely to confuse than to inform your audience.

- **Leave some blank space on each slide, and don't center everything.** Slides with significant amounts of blank space are more inviting and avoid overwhelming the audience. The empty space can appear somewhere other than the full perimeter of the slide. For example, it could be at the top of your slide or result from a wide left or right margin. Photographers and graphic design professionals have a "rule of thirds," which involves imagining a visual evenly divided into three rows and three columns.

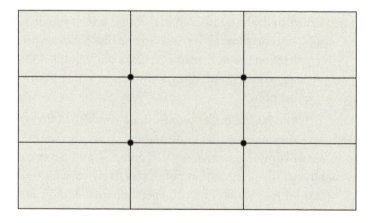

It turns out that the human eye naturally lands at the intersecting points. Those off-center points are guides to where the key element of a photograph should appear, or where you should place your text if your slide consists of a short phrase or sentence, rather than centering it. Look at digital or print advertisements and you'll see that this is how many of them are composed.

- **Use strong colors or symbols like arrows for emphasis.** Color can make a big difference in a data visualization. It also enhances text-based slides. For example, if you're showing a quotation, and there's a word or phrase you want the audience to focus on, make it a different color so it stands out. Use strongly contrasting colors, because subtle shades may not show up on all screens or in a sunny room. Given how many people have some degree of color blindness, however, you should be sure to use color only for emphasis rather than relying on it to get your point across. Other options include bolding the text you want to stand out—which you can do in combination with a contrasting color—and using a symbol like a large, thick arrow or circle to point to a key element on a slide.

- **Disclose original sources and know the story behind your numbers.** Any time you quote someone or present data, state the original source in smaller print at the bottom of your slide. It adds to your credibility and makes it easier for your audience to follow up if you've presented information that intrigues them. Do this in as few words as possible, while still providing a complete enough citation to track down the source. If you're quoting or citing someone else's work, make sure you've looked at the original source yourself, so you have a full understanding of where it comes from and what it means. You don't want to be caught off guard in the Q&A and find yourself unable to explain what the audience is seeing.

The pair of slides below illustrates how to apply these techniques. The first slide is the "before" version, which is cluttered and unappealing. To create it, I copied the text of the paragraph above on color into the most basic template generated by my office presentation software. This is what you should *not* do!

BEFORE:

Color

- Color can make a big difference in a data visualization. It also enhances text-based slides.
  - For example, if you're showing a quotation, and there's a word or phrase you want the audience to focus on, make it a different color so it stands out.
- Use strongly contrasting colors, because subtle shades may not show up on all screens or in a sunny room.
- Given how many people have some degree of color blindness, however, you should be sure to use color only for emphasis rather than relying on it to get your point across. Other options include:
  - bolding the text you want to stand out—which you can do in combination with a contrasting color—and
  - using a symbol like a large, thick arrow or circle to point to a key element on a slide.

The second slide—the "after" version—conveys the same core content in a more compelling way.

AFTER:

Color Enhances a Slide

- Color makes a word or phrase **stand out**
- Use strongly contrasting colors for bright screens and sunny rooms
- **Boldface type** and symbols like arrows and (circles) can also add emphasis ⟶

The slide has been improved in several ways:

- It has an informative title. Instead of a topic heading ("Color"), it has a statement heading ("Color Enhances a Slide"), which tells the audience what the message is.

- The default template has been replaced with a simple design that could be used throughout a full deck. The background is tinted, to avoid the glare of white slides, and the design includes two different shades of gray for the text and other slide elements. If this were a color slide, you would have even more options for creating contrast.

- The content has been pared down to the essential points, so the audience can absorb it more easily. The "before" slide contained the entire text of the original paragraph on color, presented in a maze of bullets. The "after" slide has just three crisp bullets and no subbullets.

- The headline is off-center, and there is plenty of empty space on the slide. The bullets are now separated by blank lines, and the slide does not look crowded.

- Key points are emphasized with shading variations and symbols (the arrow and circle).

Deck Structure

If you're not sure how to organize your deck, here is a simple structure you can follow. If you're delivering a creative pitch or another presentation where the element of surprise is critical, you may wish to take a different approach. But the structure outlined below works well for straightforward presentations where your goal is to make the material land and stick. It's consistent with the advice given to many professionals in business and law to "tell them what you're going to tell them, tell them, then tell them what you've told them." That structure may seem repetitive, but it creates a framework that helps your audience absorb the information and ideas you're presenting.

1. **Opening slide.** Your first slide should include a short title for your presentation, your name and organizational affiliation (no one should be left wondering who you are), and the date. Include an image if possible, because this slide is likely to remain as a backdrop while people gather and as you begin to speak. Look for an image that conveys the feeling or takeaway you want your audience to get from your presentation. If you don't have a photograph of your own or from your organization, look online for royalty-free images.

2. **Agenda slide.** This slide tells your audience what to expect by providing a list of topics you will cover or points you will make, in order. This is your opportunity to frame your presentation. If there's a bottom-line takeaway from the presentation, consider putting it on a summary slide that follows or precedes the agenda slide. Even if you're not inclined to "tell them what you're going to tell them," consider whether there's a risk that some people will leave before the presentation ends. Also, if you've distributed the full deck in advance, I guarantee people will skim through it to try to figure out the bottom line. You should be the one to tell them. For this presentation, it might be that "anyone can become a successful workplace writer," which is essentially the closing line of this book—as you may have discovered, if you too flipped to the end.

   As you present your agenda, tell the audience how long the presentation will take and make sure you don't go over. People will be watching the clock, no matter how impressive you are. If it's appropriate to do so, say how you plan to take questions: throughout the presentation; clarifying questions only during the presentation; or with all questions and reactions held until the end. The most engaging presentations involve the audience throughout, but you can judge based on your material and your audience which approach will work best.

3. **Slides with core content.** The number of content slides you prepare should be calibrated by the length of your talk and the

availability of visuals to enhance your presentation. Just keep your deck from getting too long. No one wants to watch a speaker rush through or skip over slides. It suggests poor planning and leaves the audience wondering what they missed.

4. **Transition slides.** Use transition slides to separate the core content slides, borrowing language from your agenda. These can be simple slides with just those words, or you can repurpose your agenda slide, highlighting the item you're discussing next. Consider adding a photograph or another image since, like your cover slide, transition slides can end up serving as a backdrop while you tee up a topic.

If you've prepared a long deck covering many topics, you may also want to add a navigation element to each slide, so the audience can keep track of where you are. This could be a horizontal bar at the bottom, listing each agenda item and highlighting the one you're currently discussing. It adds complexity to the design, so don't do it unless you're concerned the audience will lose the arc of your narrative. An alternative is to recap briefly throughout the presentation, with a statement in the form of "Now that I've addressed W and X, let me turn to Y before wrapping up with Z." Chapter 16 has additional suggestions for how to do this kind of road-mapping when speaking to an audience.

5. **Conclusion and next steps slide.** Don't allow your presentation to trail off. Prepare a final slide that summarizes what you want your audience to remember and lists any action steps you plan to take or are recommending to your audience.

Here is a set of sample slides. You'll see an opening slide, an agenda slide, a transition slide, and a core content slide. In this case, the core content slide is also the conclusion and next steps slide. The "after" slide above is another example of a core content slide. Slides displaying data visualizations, discussed in chapter 11, provide particularly effective content.

This opening slide includes an image that reinforces the subject of the presentation.

Topics for Today

1 | Getting started
2 | Drafting
3 | Editing
4 | Writing for public audiences

This agenda slide lists the topics that will be covered so that the audience knows what to expect.

This transition slide could be displayed when introducing or discussing a topic (in this case, the final topic on the agenda).

The simple text and icon remind the audience what is being discussed without distracting them with additional content.

Now It's Your Turn

- **Get started** with the simple steps in chapter 2.
- **Create a first draft** using the advice in chapter 3 and the examples in the book.
- **Polish it up** with the editing tips in chapter 4 and celebrate your success!

This slide shows how to present your core content in bullets—which you should do only when you can't communicate through a visual.

Presenting Your Deck

When you present a deck, your words should flow naturally. That takes practice. Be sure to practice far enough in advance that you have time to revise your deck, rather than waiting until the night before a morning presentation. A presentation you sketch out in your mind or in your notes sounds different when you try to deliver it.

There is a lively debate about whether it's best to read the text on slides verbatim or not. My view is that you should read them, rather than paraphrasing. Otherwise your audience will be reading different words than the ones you're saying aloud, which creates dueling communications channels.

If you do plan to read your slides, keeping them simple is all the more important. Wordy slides risk boring your audience, who can read faster than you can speak. Once you've read the text on the slides, you can provide additional commentary or explanation. But start with what the audience is seeing and read the text as soon as the slide appears, so the audience doesn't get ahead of you. If you can't keep your slide simple and are displaying multiple lines of text or complex images, consider using the animation or layering feature of your presentation software so you can control when each element appears.

Particularly if you're presenting your deck to a virtual audience, consider building in strategies to keep them engaged, such as posing questions in the chat or launching periodic polls. One of my favorite techniques is to ask quiz-style questions where the audience has to guess the answer, because people enjoy testing their knowledge. They're also curious about the people around them, and it will interest them to learn how others respond.

Writing for Public Audiences

Instructions and Forms

Writing clear instructions and forms requires substantial effort, but it's absolutely worth it. Think of a well-written recipe. The steps are numbered and easy to follow, and you get the tasty result the writer intended. That's the experience you want people to have when they read your instructions. Now think of the manual that came with the last appliance or device you purchased. There's a good chance it's virtually unreadable. Similarly, a well-designed form can be a cinch to complete, while a poorly designed form stirs up resentment against the company or government agency that created it.

Here are some best practices for creating these documents, followed by additional tips for forms and for instructions. The advice for writing instructions also applies to information presented in a question-and-answer format, such as an FAQ section on a website.

Best Practices

- **Whatever you do, don't go it alone.** The single most important thing is to test out your draft. Try to complete your own form or follow your own instructions, then ask your coworkers to do the same. Include people with a similar amount of background knowledge as your target audience, rather than relying solely on other technical experts. If possible, expand your usability testing beyond your organization, either through in-person focus groups or by crowdsourcing feedback online. You may wish to conduct some simple A/B testing, where you share two versions and see which performs better. You will be amazed by how much you missed, and by how much better your final version is. Whenever possible, seek input on an ongoing basis to allow for continual improvement.

- **Use language that is familiar to your audience.** Inside your organization, there may be technical terms everyone uses, but those terms are no help to readers who are unfamiliar with them. Think about the words an ordinary person would choose and use those instead. For example, during the COVID-19 global pandemic, people were told to "practice social distancing," which was an unfamiliar concept, at least at first. Far more useful were the directions to "stand at least six feet away from others" and, even more simply, "stay home." When preparing a form like an invoice, don't rely on whatever your internal accounting software automatically generates. Use recognizable terms and present the numbers in a way that is logical for your reader.

Creating Forms

- **Don't make the elements of a form too small, and consider the outliers.** Just ask anyone with the first name Christopher or Jacqueline—you need to allow enough space for the information you're requesting. This is mainly a problem with forms intended to be filled out by hand, but it can be a problem with online forms as well if they have character limits. Don't eyeball it. Try to fill out the form yourself and make sure that the font is large enough to be read easily, checkboxes can be clearly marked, and longer names, addresses, or other relevant terms fit in the allowable space using standard-sized (not cramped) handwriting. Consider which elements people might need to leave blank, such as a middle name, since not everyone has one. Likewise, ask yourself if you've given people too few options. For example, a growing number of people in the US don't consider themselves Black, Latino, white, or Asian, and need additional categories when asked for their race or ethnicity, such as Middle Eastern/North African or an option to select more than one.

- **Be consistent in your terminology.** You're going for clarity, not poetry. Don't be like my health insurance company, which asks for an "ID number" on the claims form, while my insurance card labels it the "customer number." Inconsistent terminology frustrates your reader, wastes time for customer service reps who end up fielding unnecessary inquiries, and reduces the quality of your data collection.

- **Provide examples wherever possible.** It is usually easier to work from an example than to figure out from the clues on a form what to write in a particular box or line. For example, you could put "123 Main St" in a sample address line. If you're creating an online form, you can put sample text directly into the relevant line, to be overridden when the customer starts typing.

- **Don't ask for information you don't need.** If you want to minimize errors and maximize response rates, pare your form down to the essentials. If you already have information from a customer, don't ask for it again. Consider whether you can get what you need by asking one question instead of three. If you're revising a form, ask yourself why each element is there. Some may appear for historical reasons that no longer apply given your current business process and systems.

- **Say how long it will take to complete an online form.** This is particularly important if the form cannot be easily saved and finished later. But it's a helpful courtesy no matter what the options are.

Writing Instructions

- **Don't make assumptions.** It's far better to explain too much than too little. Your readers can skip over parts they already know, but they can't fill in gaps. Pretend you don't know anything about your process or product, and think about every piece of information a person might need to be able to follow your directions.

- **Take a friendly tone.** People are following instructions because they don't know how to do something, which naturally creates anxiety. You can calm them by using simple, direct, and friendly language. You may even want to provide sympathetic cues, like "This step is the trickiest part" or "If that doesn't work, try _____." Imagine you're guiding a friend through the process, not a faceless customer.

- **If you're writing a Q&A, develop your Qs from the reader's perspective, and get right to the As.** Think about how readers will be using your product, or what questions they're most likely to have about a process, and write the questions from their perspective. When you get to the answer, make sure the first words are yes, no, or another direct response to the question posed. You can go on to explain further, but don't bury the simple answer. You want it to be easy for your customers to find the information they're seeking.

14

Writing for Media

Writing for media is something many people do at work, even if it's not part of their formal job description. If you're employed by a small organization or business that lacks a dedicated communications staff, you may be asked to pitch in and write media-friendly material from time to time. Even at a large organization with its own communications shop, you may have to review a press statement or social media post on an issue where you have particular expertise. So it helps to know the basics.

This chapter discusses how to write for journalists—through press releases and email pitches—and for social media, which may catch the attention of a journalist but is aimed at a broader audience, including potential customers and others in your industry.

Writing for Journalists

The classic form for communicating with journalists is the press release. Many organizations issue press releases to tell a story in their own words or put themselves on record. Some take an element or two of a release—such as a lead paragraph or quote—and use it in an email pitch to reporters.

A press release is a one- or two-page document that looks like a news article. The idea is to inspire journalists to share the story as you have framed it, though serious journalists will do their own writing and fact-checking and add in alternative perspectives. A press release looks like this:

Date: Month Day, Year (for example, January 1, 2022)
Contact: Name, phone, email

Headline

And Sometimes a Subheadline

GEOGRAPHIC LOCATION IN ALL CAPS.—Today, Company X announced [put the core facts here—the who/what/when/where/why].

Second paragraph with additional detail or context, to explain the significance of the announcement (so that a journalist knows why it would be timely to report on it now).

Third paragraph with a direct quote, expressed as "_____" said [name and title of person to be quoted from inside the organization], adding, "_____."

Fourth paragraph with further detail or relevant facts, which could be listed in bullets.

Optional fifth paragraph with a second quote from someone inside the organization or an expression of validation or support from outside the organization.

(indicates the end of the release)

About Company X: *Sentence or short paragraph describing the organization issuing the release and what it does. This is boilerplate language to repeat in every press release. For example*: Company X is a leader in the [describe industry] industry, with [number] locations and [number] employees, providing [describe goods/services] to [number] customers worldwide.

As always, consider your audience as you draft or review a press release. Think like a journalist and ask yourself:

- **Have you made your announcement newsworthy?** What's new here that hasn't been written about before, and why should a journalist cover this issue now? That's what they'll be wondering, and it's what their editor or producer will ask before approving a story. Identify something surprising or undiscovered and include it in your release, or look for what journalists call a news hook or a news peg. The hook could be a recent development in your industry that connects to your announcement, or a milestone like the anniversary of an important event.

- **Have you provided enough information to write a basic story?** Journalists will likely follow up to ask more detailed questions, but you can't count on that happening, so don't leave gaps in the release. If your release is backed up by a report or another public document, be sure to include a hyperlink in the release.

- **Is your quote "quotable"?** Look at the quotes in today's news—is yours similarly short and pithy? If not, cut it down until it's actually quotable. A longer quote is less appealing to a journalist. If they use it at all, they'll use just part of it, and that may not be the part you feel is most important. Avoid cliches or platitudes, which journalists will not want to quote because they won't enhance their story. And consider whom you're quoting. It should be someone readers or viewers would be interested in hearing from, which isn't always the CEO. Sometimes the best person to tell a story is the person who developed the product or led the project.

- **Is your release readable?** A press release should use similar language to a news article. Journalists don't use corporate jargon, so neither should you. When you do, you're just making their job harder, because they have to figure out how to translate what you're saying into plain English for their readers or viewers. They may decide it's not worth the effort.

Outreach to journalists often takes the form of an email pitch. The most effective pitches are tailored to individual journalists, and connect the announcement to other reporting they have done. Preparing these emails takes more time than blasting a release out to a list of reporters, but it's more likely to result in media coverage. Here's an example of what an effective email pitch looks like.

> Dear—*or*—Hi [first name of reporter],
>
> I enjoyed your recent article about _____, which _____ [say something about the impact you think it had, such as "shed light on the situation in . . ." or "helped readers understand that . . ."]. My company, _____, is announcing _____. I thought this news might interest you because _____ [explain the connection between your announcement and the article you referenced, such as "it shows how the industry is evolving to address . . ."].
>
> *Second paragraph with a little more detail or a quote that underscores the newsworthiness, such as*: Surprisingly, _____—*or*— We've discovered that _____—*or*—As _____ said, "_____."
>
> If you'd like, I can make _____ [name and title of interesting person at your organization] available for an interview [could add: "and take you on a tour of our facility" or any other opportunities you can offer to create visuals, especially if you are pitching a television or video producer instead of a print journalist].

If you've issued a press release, include a link to it in the email, as well as a phone number where the journalist can reach you.

If your goal is to react quickly to current events, another option is to put out a statement. These can be posted or excerpted on social media, but they're also often circulated to the media in a format similar to a press release, including a date, contact information, and headline. They typically open with a simple line like "[Name], [Title] at [Company Name], made the following statement today in response to [insert brief description of the event prompting the statement]:" and everything that follows is the actual quote.

Writing for Social Media

Social media allows you to become your own news organization. You can broadcast information to the public without a journalist's help, and without the critical filter they might apply to your story. That doesn't mean journalists are unimportant. They reach larger and broader audiences than most social media accounts. In fact, one reason to post on social media is to reach journalists, who rely on Twitter in particular to follow developments in the areas they cover. But social media also allows you to reach other influencers, who do their own version of reporting by sharing content through their own widely read social media channels.

Which social media platform you choose depends on the audience you want to reach and the level of engagement you're hoping to generate. Each platform has a slightly different style—some are more text-heavy, others more visual—but most involve some amount of writing.

Social media style is more informal than other kinds of writing on the job. It's more like talking than writing. Even punctuation rules get relaxed. Comma splices are more accepted, semicolons are avoided, full sentences aren't always required, and periods are often omitted. In some contexts, capitalization is used sparingly, since it can come across as unintentionally ironic. There are no hard-and-fast rules, however. The best way to judge how to write for a particular platform is to look at how others—colleagues, customers, and competitors—are expressing themselves on it.

Word limits and the average length of a post vary by platform, but less is usually more. Even after Twitter doubled its character limit from 140 to 280, the typical tweet remained well under the original limit. Often, a social media post is a single sentence, or a question and then the answer.

The key in writing for social media is to be engaging. You have to capture your audience's attention as they wade through the sea of content in their feed. Here are some strategies to make your social media post stand out.

- **Include visuals.** This could be a photograph, a chart, a light-hearted image like a GIF, or more sophisticated content like a short video or an infographic. It could even be a screenshot of a key passage from a longer report, which is also a clever way to get more words into a single post. Visuals make your content more appealing and more likely to be seen, because they are favored by the algorithms that determine which posts to display. Ideally, you should use original content that your organization has created. The quality of the image matters less than the feeling that the reader is getting an inside look or a fresh take.

- **Use humor and humility.** If what you've written sounds like corporate PR, you've missed the mark. Try to lighten up your tone, and don't be afraid to poke a little fun at yourself. You can come across as professional without sounding stuffy or boastful.

- **Engage readers directly.** You can do this by posing a question, asking for opinions, requesting feedback, or soliciting personal stories. But be prepared to monitor your account and reply as needed. You can't post and walk away if you expect people to continue to follow you.

- **Use tools like tagging others (@) and hashtags (#) to drive up readership.** If appropriate for the platform you're using, tag an organization or individual involved in the issue you're discussing to draw in their followers, or add hashtags to your post. Look for hashtags actively used by the audience you're trying to reach so you can feed into an ongoing conversation. Or you may want to create a new hashtag, for branding purposes. If you go that direction, make it distinctive, interesting, and not so long that others will struggle to repeat it. Don't feel you have to use your company name in the hashtag; it may be more effective to choose language that evokes your mission instead. For example, Kellogg's, which sells breakfast foods, branded its social media with #GreatStarts.

- **Provide a pathway to more content.** Include short links to a longer document like a report or a blog post, if the platform permits it. But don't count on readers to click through, because most won't. Include the key point you want to get across in the post itself. Some platforms allow you to create threads, which you can post simultaneously in a series, so that readers who are interested in learning more don't have to leave the platform to do so. If you are writing a thread, make sure each element makes sense on its own, because it may get shared or reposted by other people and lose context provided by the rest of the thread.

Here's an example of how you can take a finding from a lengthy document, like a report, and rewrite it into a quote to give to a journalist or a social media post. The core content doesn't change; it's just expressed differently.

REPORT: The three sectors contributing most to US greenhouse gas emissions, according to an analysis by the Environmental Protection Agency, are transportation (29% of emissions), electricity (25%), and industry (23%).

QUOTE: "The transportation sector is the number one source of greenhouse gas emissions."

SOCIAL MEDIA: Leading source of greenhouse gas emissions? Transportation. [*Include a visual—which could be a bar chart showing the three data points—and a link to the report.*]

Finally, be smart, and think before you post. Ask yourself how your organization's worst critic would respond to what you have written, including any tags, hashtags, or links. You control what you post, but you don't control the response. Make sure you don't sound small-minded or mean, and don't open yourself up to charges of hypocrisy. Ultimately, if you feel nervous about the public response, don't post. The downsides of social media do occasionally swamp the substantial upsides.

15

Commentary

Written commentary takes many forms these days. The traditional op-ed placed with a media publication is still a powerful way to communicate your views. But there are other ways to get your perspective out into the world now, including blogs, email newsletters, and a variety of online platforms. Where you choose to publish your commentary should be driven by the audience you're trying to reach and how they get their information. For example, you may wish to seek out a regional or industry publication widely read by your target audience.

No matter who your audience is or where you're publishing, there are best practices to follow when crafting your commentary. These techniques work whether you're aiming to influence public opinion, call policymakers' attention to a problem, or provide thought leadership within your industry.

- **Make sure you have an opinion to share.** Do more than just convey information; provide a perspective. John Siniff, a former opinion editor for *USA Today*, suggests this simple test: Ask yourself if anyone would disagree with what you've written. If the answer is no, you probably haven't written a thought-provoking commentary or a publishable op-ed.

- **Keep it short.** Many media outlets limit op-eds to 750 words, which is a good length even if you're self-publishing and unconstrained. Rarely is an effective commentary longer than 1000 words. Write concisely, clearly, and accessibly. More often than not, that means using shorter words, sentences, and paragraphs. Op-eds are more like newspaper articles than research papers.

- **Start and end strong.** Keep in mind that no one is required to read your commentary. You have to grab readers' attention and persuade them to stick with you. The best op-eds often start and end in the same place—with a surprising fact, a provocative question or observation, or a compelling story that draws the reader in and can be revisited to wrap the piece up and make it memorable. If you can, draw a connection to current events so your piece feels timely.

- **Cut to the chase.** Not all readers will make it to the end of your piece, so bottom line up front applies here too. Don't miss the opportunity to convey your takeaway message. It doesn't have to be in the first paragraph, but it should appear within the first 200 words.

- **Be focused and specific.** Don't try to cover too much ground—have one overarching point you want to convey. Ideally, you should be offering a fresh perspective or twist on an issue, which will be of greatest interest to your readers. If you're describing a problem, be sure to pair it with a solution, and provide concrete suggestions for what community members, policymakers, or business leaders should do in response.

- **Illustrate your argument.** You can't count on dry statistics to make your case, though if you have a few data points it may be helpful to include them. Examples and anecdotes are more likely to engage the reader. Include a personal story, if you have one that is appropriate and relevant. Or share someone else's story, so long as you have their permission to do so.

- **Briefly address notable counterarguments.** If there's an elephant in the room or conventional wisdom pointing in a different direction than the argument you are making, you don't have to linger on it, but you shouldn't ignore it. You'll be more persuasive if you acknowledge and briefly address opposing viewpoints. This is sometimes called the "to be sure" paragraph in an op-ed, though it doesn't have to include those exact words.

- **Be prepared to back up any empirical claims.** If you've written an op-ed for a major media outlet, they may fact-check it. You can make that process go more smoothly by providing hyperlinks or a separate sheet pairing each claim in your piece with a specific source.

Finally, if you're trying to publish with a media outlet, review their guidelines carefully. You'll discover

- what their word limit is (consider this nonnegotiable),
- how long they take to review a submission (which may matter if you're aiming to publish by a certain date), and
- whether they require exclusivity (meaning the op-ed can't be published anywhere else).

In general, you should only pitch one media outlet at a time. You can end up burning bridges if you submit an op-ed to one outlet for review and then allow another to publish it before the first outlet's review window has lapsed.

Expect that they will edit your op-ed after it is accepted, though you should still submit a polished piece. Opinion editors are unlikely to be interested in a rough draft. Media outlets also usually determine the headline, though it can help to submit your piece with a suggested headline.

16

Public Speaking

Any time you address a group of people, you're engaged in public speaking. You may be able to pull it off without extensive preparation, especially if you are talking briefly about a topic you know well to a familiar audience. But it always helps to have something written out in advance, even if you don't plan to speak from a script.

This chapter begins by explaining how to craft short, clear talking points, which may be all you need. Talking points are also one of the most versatile writing forms. Once you have written them, you can adapt them into many other kinds of documents. The chapter then guides you through the process of writing out and delivering a full set of remarks, including a formal speech, and closes with a brief discussion of how to incorporate visuals.

Talking Points

Talking points are crisp, clear statements presented in bullet form. A well-written set of talking points can be used verbatim to present an idea or discuss an issue, empowering you to walk into any setting and start speaking sensibly and thoughtfully.

Writing out your talking points also forces you to think through the argument you're making or the explanation you're providing. The task of organizing your ideas into a limited set of bullet points focuses you on identifying the most persuasive or informative ones. As a bonus, once you've done the work of creating talking points, they function as boilerplate material for other forms of writing. That could be a short email or a lengthier memo or report, where your talking points become the subheadings that guide the reader through the piece. Talking points can also serve as the script for presenting a slide deck.

How long should talking points be? A page or less per topic. If you're using them to answer questions, all you'll likely need are a few top-line bullets, perhaps accompanied by additional background information, such as statistics you want to have at your fingertips. Leave enough blank space on the page to allow for a quick skim to find the relevant point and use at least a 14-point font for easier reading. Here is the format I like to use.

TALKING POINT BASICS

- **Put the most important points at the top.** This mitigates the risk that you will get cut off before making a critical argument.

- **Talking points are presented in bullets, like this.** They are often just one sentence, but they can be a few sentences (three at most). The lead sentence should be in bold and state the key point, with any additional sentences providing backup.

- **Talking points should be easy to understand and read aloud.** Use plain language and simple sentence structure. Avoid unnecessary detail.

- **Each point should stand on its own.** You should be able to pluck any bullet from the page and use it without reference to the others.

If you're having trouble getting going on your talking points, try to write an elevator pitch instead. This is the 1-minute (120-to-150-word) speech you'd give if you found yourself riding in an elevator with someone you wanted to influence. I've found that many people are more comfortable crafting an elevator pitch than talking points, perhaps because it feels less formal and more conversational. Once you have your elevator pitch written, dig through it for the key points, put dots in front of them, and you've got a draft of your talking points.

It works both ways—once you've drafted talking points, you're ready to make a pitch. Set a 1-minute timer and try to use your talking points to sell your idea or explain your issue. If it flows naturally, you're all set. If you find yourself wanting to make other points or use different language once you're in elevator pitch mode, revise your talking points.

Written Remarks

Even if you're delivering a brief set of remarks and not a full-blown speech, you may be more comfortable having the full text written out in advance. You may not read every word on the page precisely as written, but the safety net it provides is reassuring. If you get nervous or momentarily forget what you had planned to say, you can glance down and it's all there waiting for you.

Begin the writing process by considering what you want the takeaway from your remarks to be. What do you want the audience to leave thinking about, and remember afterward? That's your North Star, and it should shine through your text. You can give it an extra lift with a cue like, "If you remember one thing. . . ."

Next, think about the structure of your remarks. A speech is not a series of facts and observations loosely strung together. It's a journey you take with your audience, whether to inform, inspire, or persuade. To keep them engaged on that journey, you need a narrative arc to pull them in and keep them with you through the end. Here are a few techniques for constructing a narrative arc.

- **Tap into your audience's imagination.** "Imagine" is one of the most powerful words in the dictionary, as communications consultant Frank Luntz has observed. It's a terrific way to begin a speech. "Imagine a world where _____", "Imagine a product that _____," or "Imagine if every employee at this firm _____" invites your audience to start dreaming and thinking with you. You may want to pause briefly, to allow them to begin imagining on their own, and then proceed with the rest of your remarks, which should take the audience on the journey of how to make the dream a reality. You can also open by describing a situation you want to change ("Right now, our customers feel _____") and then pivot to "Now imagine if _____."

- **Tell the beginning of a story and return to it at the end.** If you have a story that illustrates the takeaway message in your speech, use it. Scientists have found that hearing a story releases chemicals in our brains that keep us engaged and help us form memories. Begin your remarks by telling just the first half of the story, so your audience starts to wonder, "What happened to that person/company/town?" That creates the element of suspense fundamental to good storytelling. As you wrap up your remarks, resolve the suspense and share how the story ends, completing the narrative arc. Your story doesn't have to be about an actual customer or product, though a case study can be effective. Your story can operate as a metaphor, as children's stories often do. We learn from the "Three Little Pigs" to work hard and build wisely, not that talking wolves can blow down houses. Consider whether you've heard a story that stirs up the feelings you want your audience to have and resolves them in a way that reinforces your takeaway message.

- **Share confidences or experiences.** Another way to draw your audience in is to share a confession, or an experience they're likely to relate to. "I'm going to let you in on a little secret" or "Have you ever _____?" makes the audience feel connected to you and interested in what you have to say next.

- **Pose a question.** One of the simplest ways to build a narrative arc is to pose a question to your audience at the outset that you answer by the end. A "why" question works particularly well in this context ("Why has _____ been so successful?" or "Why have we struggled to _____, and what can we do about it?").

However you construct your narrative arc, be sure to capture the audience's attention right away. Don't burn through those valuable opening minutes by talking about event logistics or thanking all the people involved. Resist the temptation to tell the audience about the nerves you're feeling or the process of crafting your remarks. Starting with "when I sat down to write this speech" risks putting your audience to sleep. Get their attention by diving right into what you're there to say.

Your closing should be similarly strong. Wrap up on a positive or hopeful note, and find a way to issue or repeat a call for action if that's part of your message ("So let's work together to _____"). Make sure your audience leaves with a sense of what they can do about the topic you've discussed.

Once you have identified your takeaway message and the beginning and end of your narrative arc, you're ready to fill in the rest. Exactly what you write depends on what you want to communicate, but here are a few best practices to follow in drafting your remarks.

- **Identify the key points you want to make.** Create a bullet outline to follow as you write, so your speech has a solid structure and doesn't meander.

- **Find words you can lean on and repeat.** Speeches are like poetry—they are supposed to lift us out of ourselves for a moment. Just as poetry is often punctuated with repeated words and phrases, so are many of the great speeches. Martin Luther King Jr. repeated the phrase "I have a dream that one day . . ." five times in his famous speech, each time painting a fresh picture of the future he imagined. It was lyrical and memorable. The tone of your remarks may be less aspirational, but you can still use this technique. For example, try repeating a phrase like "If we take this bold step" or "Here's what we know." Or look for opportunities to use parallel construction, where you structure your sentences or phrases the same way. It could be a simple subject and verb ("We can," "We must," "We will") or a string of adjectives ("We will come out of this stronger, healthier, and wiser"). Remember, all the audience has to guide them is their ears; they can't go back and reread a confusing passage. The repetition or parallelism helps them stay with you and recall what you said afterward.

- **Think of yourself as a storyteller, even when you are talking about numbers.** If you are speaking about a technical subject or sharing data, wrap a narrative around it to help the audience absorb what you're saying. Instead of rattling off a string of numbers, explain the relevance of each data point or empirical finding you cite, so your audience has a framework to put it in. Otherwise you risk the audience misunderstanding you, or misinterpreting the information you're providing and drawing their own conclusions.

- **If you use humor, do it authentically.** It can help to use humor when you speak, if you're comfortable doing so. Putting a smile on people's faces warms them up. Just be careful to do it in a way that is true to who you are, without offending or turning off your audience. One of the most hackneyed speech-writing techniques is to hunt around for a joke and pop it into your remarks. It nearly always falls flat because it feels forced. But a funny anecdote or a humorous aside—especially if they make the audience feel good about themselves—can be an effective way to connect and make your speech more memorable.

- **Remember that it's always about them, never about you.** You don't engage people by talking about yourself, but rather about how your topic affects them. One way to ensure you've stayed true to that principle is to search your draft for the words "I" and "me," and delete them wherever possible. "You" and "we" (if the "we" includes the audience) are much better. In addition, look for opportunities to involve your audience directly. A simple technique is to suggest, "Raise your hand if you have ever _____," which has the added bonus of getting your audience interested in the people around them, as they look to see how others have responded.

How long should you speak? Aim for 20 minutes or less. You want to leave your audience excited and engaged, not praying for you to release them. There's a reason TED Talks are limited to 18 minutes. Even if you're asked to speak longer, see if you can negotiate down to 20 minutes. Terrific speeches, and even commencement addresses, have been delivered in less time. As Kenneth Roman and Joel Raphaelson wryly observed in their classic *Writing That Works*, "On your way out after a speech, do you remember ever thinking it was good—but a little too short?"

Finally, be sure to practice delivering your remarks. Words flow differently on the page than when spoken aloud, and practicing makes your delivery more effective. Here is some advice to keep in mind as you rehearse.

- **Speak slowly.** Time yourself, and aim for 120–150 words per minute. This may feel slow, especially if you ordinarily talk quickly. I promise your audience will be grateful.

- **Have your first line nailed.** Memorize your opening sentence, especially if you're speaking from an outline or talking points. Back when he was in private practice arguing cases, Chief Justice John Roberts would write at the top of his notes, "Mr. Chief Justice and may it please the Court," even though every first-year law student knows that's how you're supposed to begin a Supreme Court argument. He just didn't want to panic and end up stumbling through his opening line. More generally, the better you know your speech, the better you'll be able to connect with your audience, because you'll be looking out at them and not constantly lowering your gaze to the page in front of you.

- **Learn how to pronounce any proper names or difficult words you plan to use.** Spell them out phonetically in your written text, so you don't forget when it comes time to deliver the remarks. For example, my last name is pronounced "COH-venn." About half of the people who introduce me get this right, and I'm always pleased when they do. You can also lose credibility if you are presenting yourself as an expert but mispronounce the name of a location, company, or product—or even a word in the English language. Particularly if you are a big reader, your vocabulary may include words you've never heard spoken aloud. That's fine if you're using them in your writing, but it can be embarrassing if you try to pronounce them for the first time in front of an audience.

- **Make eye contact with individuals in the audience.** Connecting with individual people makes your remarks feel like an engaging conversation, not a dull lecture. That doesn't mean your eyes should be constantly darting about the room. Pick an individual and land your gaze on that person for a couple of sentences—enough to express a thought—and then move on to someone else and do the same thing.

- **Consider adding gestures.** You can use simple gestures without seeming theatrical. An effective technique is to use your hands as road maps and signposts. State at the outset that you're going to talk about three things, and as you name them, anchor each in the space around you. For example, if you were talking about the elements of the triple bottom line, you could gesture to the left and say "profit," put your hands in front of you and say "people," and gesture to the right as you say "planet." That's the road map to the journey. Then, as you transition to talking about each topic, put your hands in the proper place ("Next, let's consider how this will affect the people in our community," pointing straight ahead with your hands). Those are the signposts, signaling to your audience where they are on the journey. It comes across much more naturally than you might think.

- **Record a dry run and make yourself watch it.** There's nothing more humbling or helpful than watching a replay of yourself speaking. But don't be too hard on yourself. Focus on the rough spots so you can smooth them out, and notice if you lean on a filler word like "um" or "like." Many of us do, and it can be distracting. You can break the habit within weeks with the help of a family member or coworker, by asking them to nudge you every time you use your filler word. Once you've rid your speech of these words, you may pause more often. Embrace those brief silences. They give the listener a moment to process what you've said, just as you need a moment to consider what to say next.

Using Visuals When You Speak

A carefully selected image can enhance your presentation by evoking the emotions you want your audience to experience, which could be anything from compassion or concern to excitement or inspiration. You could also play a short video clip, to set the mood or tell part of your story.

The most effective backdrops are photographs. They don't require the audience to read and therefore don't create cognitive dissonance. That said, slides with words are expected in some professional settings, and you may feel you have to use them. If you do use slides, be sure to pause and give your audience a moment to absorb each of them before proceeding with your remarks.

For more complete guidance on how to prepare and present data visualizations and slide decks, see chapters 11 and 12.

Conclusion

In the digital age, the words we write shape our professional identities. They can either propel us forward in our careers or hold us back.

If you put in the effort, your colleagues will eagerly read your posts and emails, your managers will be persuaded by your memos, your clients will appreciate your decks and reports, and the public will value your commentary.

Best of all, after a while, it won't feel like effort. And once workplace writing starts to come more naturally, you can put to better use the time you previously spent hunched over a keyboard, struggling to complete a writing task.

Even the most accomplished writers need ongoing sources of inspiration. If you find yourself hungry for fresh examples of good writing, pull up the front page or editorial page of a nationally ranked newspaper. The best journalists show us every day how to clearly explain complex situations. That's their business model, and it can be yours too.

With the ideas gathered from this book and continued practice, I am confident you can become a successful workplace writer and communicator.

Acknowledgments

It's always best to start at the beginning, as a good witch once advised, so let me start by thanking the people who raised me. My mother, Carol Wood, taught me from an early age to love reading and to appreciate good writing of all kinds. My father, Ethan Coven, taught me to pay attention to spelling and has earned his Grammar Police badge many times over. And my sister, Emily Coven, is a creative and talented writer. All three of them read and commented on my manuscript, for which I am grateful.

The other early influences in my life were my teachers. I learned to write in the public schools of Middletown, Connecticut, guided and supported by inspiring teachers. Alexander Tucci taught me not only how to develop a thesis and points of proof for an argument, but also to strive for excellence in every piece of writing. The late Jim Bransfield encouraged me to try writing features for the school newspaper, and didn't bat an eye when I turned in articles on topics like how to create "big hair" (it was the 1980s). My teachers helped me believe in myself, which is one of the greatest gifts you can give a child.

Over the course of my career, I have learned from many people about the craft of good writing—far too many to name. I want to give two special shout-outs, however. The first goes to my longtime boss and mentor, Bob Greenstein, who pursued clarity and precision in writing with an unwavering determination. Tacked to my office wall for many years was the only paper he ever returned to me with just a single line edit. The second shout-out goes to my

White House colleague Taryn Toyama, who introduced me to the magical phrase "bottom line up front."

I particularly want to thank the Princeton School of Public and International Affairs, including former dean Ceci Rouse, for ushering me into the classroom. I have treasured the opportunity to learn with and from the students in my writing classes and workshops as well as from my colleagues on the faculty and staff. Those experiences inspired me to write this book. I was also lucky to have the chance to try out an early draft on the students in a communications course I cotaught at NYU Law with Lily Batchelder.

My deep appreciation goes to the friends and colleagues who reviewed all or part of my manuscript, drawing on their professional experiences across a host of fields—including finance, health, hospitality, law, media, and technology—to provide excellent feedback that made this book stronger. They include Stacy Beck, Shannon Buckingham, Ken Crawford, Gerry Hackett, Steve Hudak, Dave Hung, Patrick Kerley, Cathy Kim, Jon Schwabish, Ian Shapira, John Siniff, and Cathy Young. I'm also grateful to the people who advised me on the mysterious process of book publishing, including Sarah Pinneo, Lauren Emerson, Jenni Anderson, Eliza Rosenberry, and the late Alan Krueger. Marilyn Moller gave me invaluable feedback on my book proposal and early drafts of several chapters. And special thanks go to Erick Messer for his design assistance.

The wizard behind this book was Peter Dougherty. I wandered into the Princeton University Press offices in the spring of 2018, in search of someone to advise me on a kernel of a book idea, and had the great fortune to be referred to Peter. From our first lunch meeting, he gave me superb advice, and when he later offered to recommend this book to his editorial board, I knew it had found the right home. Peter also enlisted an accomplished group of writing instructors to review an early draft of the manuscript. This final version incorporates many of the suggestions in their thorough and thoughtful reports.

Finally, let me thank the three companions who hung with me through every twist and turn of the yellow brick road: my husband, Paul Frick, and my children, Noah and Daphne. I first met Paul when I was still learning to write on the job, and he is the person who taught me how to write a good memo. I'm regularly struck by his creative talent, and I'm grateful for the support and encouragement he has given me over the years and throughout this project. Noah and Daphne make me laugh, think, and strive every day to be the best parent I can be. They regularly asked how the book was going and listened attentively to my reply. My own Toto, Skipper the spaniel, faithfully snoozed at my feet throughout the many drafts and revisions. I don't know if it's possible to write a book without a dog by your side, and I don't want to find out.

Notes

Chapter 1. Developing a Professional Style

p. 8: "**most adults in the US are not highly proficient readers**": US Department of Education, "Adult Literacy in the United States," July 2019, nces.ed.gov /pubs2019/2019179.pdf.

p. 8: "**Warren Buffett always wrote the annual Berkshire Hathaway shareholder letter as if the audience were his sisters**": Emmie Martin, "Warren Buffett Writes His Annual Letter as if He's Talking to His Sisters—Here's Why," CNBC, February 25, 2019, www.cnbc.com/2019/02/25/why-warren -buffett-writes-his-annual-letter-like-it-is-for-his-sisters.html.

p. 9: "**Advertising executives Kenneth Roman and Joel Raphaelson . . . suggest making 'a conscious effort not to insult people'**": Kenneth Roman and Joel Raphaelson, *Writing That Works: How to Communicate Effectively in Business* (New York: HarperCollins, 2000), 151.

Chapter 2. Getting Started

p. 10: "**Stephen King observed in his memoir that 'the scariest moment is always just before you start'**": Stephen King, *On Writing: A Memoir of the Craft* (New York: Scribner, 2000), 269.

p. 10: "**'Go away from it,' Nobel laureate Toni Morrison once advised**": Elissa Schappell and Claudia Brodsky Lacour, "Toni Morrison, The Art of Fiction No. 134," *Paris Review*, Fall 1993, www.theparisreview.org/interviews/1888 /the-art-of-fiction-no-134-toni-morrison.

Chapter 3. Writing a First Draft

p. 14: "**The federal plain language guidelines . . . describe three types of headings**": Plain Language Action and Information Network, "Federal Plain Language Guidelines: Revision 1," May 2011, www.plainlanguage.gov/media /FederalPLGuidelines.pdf, 11.

p. 15: "**Gary Provost illustrated this point beautifully**": Gary Provost, *100 Ways to Improve Your Writing* (New York: Mentor, 1985), 60–61.

p. 16: "**Lynne Truss explains that a comma 'tells the reader how to hum the tune'**": Lynne Truss, *Eats, Shoots & Leaves* (New York: Gotham Books, 2003), 71.

p. 16: "**consider this description of two formulas for measuring inflation**": Adapted from US Bureau of Labor Statistics, "Frequently Asked Questions about the Chained Consumer Price Index for All Urban Consumers (C-CPI-U)," last modified December 20, 2019, www.bls.gov/cpi/additional-resources/chained-cpi-questions-and-answers.htm#Question_2.

p. 18: "**as damaging as smoking fifteen cigarettes a day**": Health Resources & Services Administration, "The 'Loneliness Epidemic,'" last modified January 2019, www.hrsa.gov/enews/past-issues/2019/january-17/loneliness-epidemic.

p. 18: "**The Irish musician Bono persuaded religious conservatives**": G. Richard Shell and Mario Moussa, *The Art of Woo: Using Strategic Persuasion to Sell Your Ideas* (New York: Penguin Books, 2007), 112–13.

Chapter 4. Editing

p. 20: "**In author E. B. White's introduction**": William Strunk Jr. and E. B. White, *The Elements of Style* (Upper Saddle River, NJ: Pearson Education, 2000), xv.

p. 29: "**Pity the Postal Service employee who approved a stamp honoring the poet Maya Angelou**": Lonnae O'Neal, "Book Author Joan Walsh Anglund Says of Angelou Stamp: 'That's My Quote,'" *Washington Post*, April 6, 2015, www.washingtonpost.com/lifestyle/style/book-author-joan-walsh-anglund-claims-angelou-quote-on-stamp/2015/04/06/62d31934-dcc8-11e4-acfe-cd057abefa9a_story.html.

Chapter 6. Memos

p. 53: "**Amazon executive Jeff Bezos once observed**": Jeffrey P. Bezos, "2017 Letter to Shareholders," April 18, 2018, www.aboutamazon.com/news/company-news/2017-letter-to-shareholders.

Chapter 11. Data Visualizations

p. 79: "**consumers are more likely to believe**": Aner Tal, "Beware the Truthiness of Charts," *Harvard Business Review*, November 19, 2015, www.hbr.org/2015/11/beware-the-truthiness-of-charts.

Chapter 14. Writing for Media

p. 105: "**Even after Twitter doubled its character limit from 140 to 280, the typical tweet remained well under the original limit**": Jacob Kastrenakes, "Twitter Says People Are Tweeting More, but Not Longer, with 280-Character Limit," *The Verge*, February 8, 2018, www.theverge.com/2018/2/8/16990308/twitter-280-character-tweet-length.

p. 107: "**The three sectors contributing most to US greenhouse gas emissions**": US Environmental Protection Agency, "Sources of Greenhouse Gas Emissions," accessed June 25, 2021, www.epa.gov/ghgemissions/sources-greenhouse-gas-emissions.

Chapter 15. Commentary

p. 108: "**John Siniff . . . suggests this simple test**": John Siniff, email to author, February 28, 2021.

Chapter 16. Public Speaking

p. 113: "**'Imagine' is one of the most powerful words in the dictionary, as communications consultant Frank Luntz has observed**": Dr. Frank Luntz, *Words That Work: It's Not What You Say, It's What People Hear* (New York: Hachette Books, 2007), 241.

p. 114: "**Scientists have found that hearing a story releases chemicals in our brains**": Lani Peterson, "The Science behind the Art of Storytelling," *Harvard Business School Publishing Corporate Learning Blog*, November 14, 2017, www.harvardbusiness.org/the-science-behind-the-art-of-storytelling/.

p. 117: "**As Kenneth Roman and Joel Raphaelson wryly observed . . . 'On your way out after a speech'**": Roman and Raphaelson, *Writing That Works*, 108.

p. 117: "**Chief Justice John Roberts . . . would write**": Joan Biskupic, *The Chief: The Life and Turbulent Times of Chief Justice John Roberts* (New York: Hachette Book Group, 2020), 120–21.

p. 118: "**An effective technique is to use your hands as road maps and signposts**": This recommendation follows advice given by Nancy Houfek, the former head of voice and speech at Harvard University's American Repertory Theater, in a training on "The Art of Presentation."

Index